# Chase the Rainbow

# Chase the Rainbow

# POORNA
# BELL

**SIMON &
SCHUSTER**

London · New York · Sydney · Toronto · New Delhi

A CBS COMPANY

First published in Great Britain by Simon & Schuster UK Ltd, 2017
A CBS COMPANY

p.v: images © KTB Wedding Photography

1 3 5 7 9 10 8 6 4 2

Simon & Schuster UK Ltd
1st Floor
222 Gray's Inn Road
London WC1X 8HB

www.simonandschuster.co.uk
www.simonandschuster.com.au
www.simonandschuster.co.in

Simon & Schuster Australia, Sydney
Simon & Schuster India, New Delhi

The author and publishers have made all reasonable efforts
to contact copyright-holders for permission, and apologise
for any omissions or errors in the form of credits given.
Corrections may be made to future printings.

A CIP catalogue record for this book
is available from the British Library

Hardback ISBN: 978-1-4711-6069-1
Trade paperback ISBN: 978-1-4711-6070-7
eBook ISBN: 978-1-4711-6071-4

Typeset in Garamond by M Rules
Printed and bound by CPI Group (UK) Ltd, Croydon, CR0 4YY

MIX
Paper from
responsible sources
FSC® C020471

Simon & Schuster UK Ltd are committed to sourcing paper
that is made from wood grown in sustainable forests and support the Forest
Stewardship Council, the leading international forest certification organisation.
Our books displaying the FSC logo are printed on FSC certified paper.

*Rob, this is your song.*

*Chase the Rainbow* is a game-changing book. Poorna Bell's moving account of the pressures on modern men could be a life-saver. This is a brave and bold work that will inspire us all to talk openly and honestly about depression once and for all. Everyone should read this book.

ARIANNA HUFFINGTON

*This isn't a love story that ends in a kiss at sunset. It isn't one where love is more powerful than the universe.*

*It is one where love was strong, endured a storm so bad it almost destroyed everything; where it forgave, was deep and true, and where it remembers and was honoured.*

*But it's not one where love wins the fight.*

*In this story, a boy meets a girl. Their first date is a sushi restaurant; the warmth of dim sum and tempura blowing steam and condensation against the wintery cold outside.*

*The boy shares his love of smoky Caravaggio paintings, newts, plants, birds – every living thing that crawls, runs and swims across the face of the planet is given his admiration (barring slugs – he definitely doesn't like slugs).*

*He tells her he loves her, he wants to marry her, he can imagine their International Beige babies (he is creamy white, she is brown like a nut); he shows her his favourite flower: sweet-smelling freesias that he brings to her door.*

*In spring he buys her daffodils almost every day because he delights in waking up next to the buttery yellow petals that brighten her bedroom table.*

*The girl falls in love – how could she not?*

*This boy is the kindest person she has ever met.*

*So she looks only at the light because it is blinding and it is bliss, and she doesn't see the darkness he is desperately trying to hide. If she sees it, he thinks, she will turn away in disgust and not love him any more.*

*Not understanding she would love him to the ends of the earth.*

*So the boy marries the girl, and after the streamers are packed away and the thank-you notes sent out, he spends the next three years in bed.*

*He sweats, he tosses, he cries, he turns. He is being eaten by a demon that is slowly taking everything away from him, as if it is a game of chess and he is the pawn.*

*When it has him open, vulnerable and alone, it will move in swiftly when he is at his most defenceless.*

*And then one day, the boy stops crying. He stops fighting. He spends his last day in a state of calm happiness. He knows he loves the girl. He knows he loves his family. But love has nothing to do with it.*

*He tells them he loves them, but he cannot stay. He cannot live with the person he has become.*

*And so the boy takes himself away into a winter's night. And amid the sound of insects, the murmur of birds roosting in the trees, he goes to the woods, and he slips the noose around his neck.*

*He looks the darkness in the eye. They both nod, because they knew it would always end this way but, man, did he put up a good fight.*

*He has been here before, many times. He has seen the door, many times. But this time, there is no looking away. There are no last words.*

*He takes the love everyone has given him and leaves it at his feet. There is only the door, and he steps through with relief in his heart.*

*And so begins our grief.*

# Chapter One

'Hello? Hello? Are you still there?'

I was going to kill my friend Tania. Most people in January are busy squeezing themselves into gym kit they won't use again come February, signing up for online dating after shucking off a bad relationship, or self-flagellating in the pub because they've failed to quit drinking.

While most nations use the start of the New Year for positive new beginnings, we Brits love to turn it into an existential crisis.

The reason why Tania's days were numbered is because I specifically told her that 2009 was going to be the Year of Me. No more dating, no more bozos, and perhaps I'd finally set up that nunnery I kept talking about.

So what did she do? She sent me two things without fore-warning: 1) a bottle of horny goat weed pills in the post and 2) an email to me and her Kiwi friend Rob introducing us to each other.

I mean, *Jesus wept, Tania, it was January.* And not just any time in January, *mid*-January – that crotch of the year when you have no money, your diet has gone down the shitter, and you still have ten weeks of winter left to go.

It was cold, raining and dark, and I, like most women, tended to grow body hair for extra warmth and sport gnarled, horny toenails like that old Indian guy in *The Guinness Book of World Records* because I wouldn't be wearing sandals anytime soon.

I didn't want to leave the confines of my cosy home. I didn't want to have to dust off my Gillette Venus razor and fish out the nail clippers. And if I was disinclined to do this before I called my blind date, then I was doubly disinclined after I had talked to him on the phone.

He spoke with such deep, long pauses – at the last count nearly six seconds had passed between sentences – that I was concerned he might have a medical problem. Plus, his accent didn't help – beyond making out a few words like 'Friday' and 'sushi', I couldn't understand a word he was saying.

I mean, how concerned should I be? Did he have narco-lepsy? Was he going to fall face first into his salmon nigiri during the date and I'd have to revive him by being inventive with chopsticks?

'Hello?' Ten more seconds of this and then I was cutting him off.

I had started the year with my traditional New Year's Day missive to myself in a new diary, which usually was written hungover, full of promises of what I would and wouldn't do. This year had been no different but it had a particular tone – I had reached my limit of dating men who didn't deserve my affections.

> I wish I could start a diary for once feeling like the sunshine was bursting out of my arse, but in keeping with tradition, that is unfortunately not the case. I'm getting over a broken heart (again).
>
> I'm just wondering when any of it is going to work out and I keep dreaming of my soulmate but getting no closer to finding him in real life.

It may not have been the stuff of Shakespeare but Silent Bob on the phone here was not presenting himself as soulmate material.

The truth of the matter was that, although I pretended to be a hard-drinking tomboy who didn't care about being rejected, I secretly wrote Dear Diary entries about how I believed in true love.

Alongside the gig ticket stubs were flowers I pressed in the folds, as if they would breathe substance into a silent wish. As with anyone who wants love in their life, what I wanted was to be seen, the good and bad, my limitations and potential, and for that person to unconditionally love what they saw.

When I sobered up, I wrote another entry shortly afterwards.

I wait for a love so big it lives in every part of my life. Where the morning becomes a moment of quiet peace and entangled limbs; body upon body in a loving sprawl.

I wait for the man who can see beyond my skin and really looks into me. He is out there, he has to be. Only a big love will make me lie still.

It wasn't that I thought I was unlovable, but I knew it was going to have to take someone exceptional to deal with the type of woman I was. Especially since I came from a family of crazy lady warrior types, who were both fearless and vulnerable, immense fun yet unreasonable and in need of grounding. We needed men who earthed us but didn't bore the pants off us at the same time.

'Hello? Christ, are you still there?'

'Yeeeeeeessss.' He sounded like the whale from *Finding Nemo*, except in this scenario I was Marlin, not Dory, and I didn't know what the fuck he was saying.

'Just email me.' I put the phone down.

While I would later find out that Rob had been on the tail end of a three-day party when we first spoke, burned out and bonged up, I discovered he was much better on email.

Like me, he was a journalist, but, unlike me, he didn't strap on a pregnancy suit to find out whether people would give up a seat on the Tube, run around a cryo chamber in a bikini to see if his extremities would freeze or visit a woman who deciphered the future from coffee grounds.

This guy actually knew stuff and wrote about the environment. He spoke at conferences. It wasn't just his profession that made him different from the guys I normally dated (they tended to be DJs or personal trainers – all emotionally unavailable and poor); he wasn't shy about showing me he was interested.

I had just finished my first travel commission at the *Guardian* as a freelance writer, and my piece on kayaking around Kerala was due out a few days before our first date.

'Congratulations on the "throwing fag butts at dolphins" line,' Rob wrote.

I was touched that he'd gone out and bought a paper.

Rob worked mainly as a trade journalist and wanted to branch into consumer journalism.

'It's not that I don't enjoy writing about the environment (apart from air pollution, I hate air pollution),' he wrote, 'and I even really like my other regular contract, which is a little publication on land contamination (sexy, huh?), which is a rather fiendish combination of ecology, chemistry, toxicology and politics. Oh dear, I think my inner science nerd is exposed.'

He was funny as well as clever.

Tania made the mistake of assuming we had forgiven her for the blind date email and asked our opinion on this guy who couldn't tell the difference between 'into' and 'in to'.

'People who can't spell are crap in the sack. Scientific fact,' wrote Rob.

Tania wrote back sometime later in the week to tell us that a quick search revealed this guy was actually married.

'Aha,' replied Rob.

'You said crap in the sack, not morally crap,' Tania fired back.

'Same thing.'

During our email exchanges, he also asked me on a second date to a restaurant opening before we'd even had our first date, something that normally would have sent me running had he not caveated it with 'assuming we don't hate each other on sight'. I said no.

Charming and witty though he seemed, I still wasn't convinced this would be a goer.

Especially when – in my ignorance of confusing New Zealand with Australia – I thought I was going to get some young, tousle-haired, blond surfer from *Home and Away*, and what I got – according to the picture Rob sent so we'd recognise each other on our date – was a skinhead in a Celtic t-shirt cuddling his gigantic dog Daisy.

I didn't hate dogs, but after an Alsatian bit my mother on the arse when I was a child, I wasn't enamoured with them either. And Daisy – a mix of pit bull, mastiff and boxer – looked like she ate arses for breakfast.

We met in Fujiyama, tucked away in the backstreets of Brixton. A night sharp with cold, streetlights shining halos where it greeted the mist from our mouths.

My flatmate and best friend Mal dropped me off, and I bitched the entire way about how this guy was just going to be another bozo. 'Or he's going to wear flip-flops to the date, like that last guy did.'

I refused to get out of the car, clutching onto my seatbelt for dear life. When Mal finally prised my fingers from the dashboard and booted me out, I knew there was no going back. Mainly because she sped off the moment my feet hit tarmac.

It is funny when you look back on first meetings. I had met men who immediately set off Roman candles and fizzing sparklers. And they lasted all of two seconds.

Rob was something much slower than that. He looked like a man carved by sea, sun and earth. Broad shoulders, thick forearms. A long nose and a strong jaw.

Crinkly around the eyes when he smiled, like lines drawn lightly in sand, a close-shaved head that made him look tough and lean, but when you looked closer, you saw softness in his eyes.

He got up when he saw me approach the table, and he stood up when I went to the bathroom. This was that mythical chivalry thing we'd heard so much about while learning Jane Austen by rote.

We ordered cold Tiger beer because it was steaming hot inside the restaurant. When he removed his sweatshirt, his t-shirt stuck to it and rode up to his neck, showing me the most perfectly toned, creamy white torso. That was unexpected.

Thankfully, my jaw dropped while he was still navigating his shirt over his face. Then we talked and talked.

Despite my initial cynicism, I had a good time. Rob was unlike any person I had ever been on a date with. He didn't look like the men I usually went for (apart from his strong nose, I loved that. Oh, and the flat torso). And he certainly didn't act like most of the men I normally went for.

'Good morning, dear, I hope you had a good time,' came the message the following day. Normally, if a guy sent me a message (*if*), it would come so late I could have already been dead and nostril-deep in a bowl of cornflakes for all they knew.

We talked about our second date. 'The only thing that crossed my mind,' he said, 'was a classical gig if there was anything decent on, as you said you'd never been to one.'

Brownie points for paying attention but I didn't want anything too stuffy.

As it was my turn to arrange the date and I knew he liked music, we spent date number two drinking rum on ice, watching an old (literally old – they were each pushing eighty) folk band in a now-defunct bar on Tottenham Court Road.

It was a risk – I knew he was all Fugazi, Turbonegro and The Specials – but this was the only gig on that night, and it turned out he had a huge soft spot for country and western.

As the evening went on, I wondered whether he was going to kiss me. There he was, rabbiting on about James Taylor, and I looked at his mouth. A thin line on top, a fuller lip below.

I didn't know if I wanted Rob to kiss me. I mean sure, I already knew I loved talking to him, but I hadn't had a semi-sober first kiss for a long time.

Plus, my last one had gone terribly wrong.

It was with some guy I met on (another) blind date and it felt like a washing machine had gone sentient and was trying to run a spin cycle via my mouth.

By the time Rob and I left the bar, there wasn't even a hint of puckering up. In my head, I had already decided there wasn't going to be a third date if the guy couldn't summon up the nerve.

We took a black cab back to mine, with the intention that it would drop him home in neighbouring Streatham straight afterwards. 'Two stops,' I told the driver firmly.

As we neared my flat in Balham, Rob was seized by a mysterious urge to urinate.

'Honestly,' he said, 'I know what this looks like but I really, really need to use the toilet.'

We let the cab go. I felt heartless kicking him out immediately, so we sat on Mal's black leather sofa, had a nightcap and talked some more.

He was from a Catholic middle-class family in Auckland; I was from a Hindu middle-class family based in Kent by way of Bangalore.

'So what degree did you do?' I asked.

He looked at his glass. 'I didn't.'

'But, you're a journalist?'

'Yep. I quit school at sixteen. Worked as a bartender, landscape gardener, truck driver. Took a six-month course when I was twenty-five and retrained as a journalist.'

'And you own your own house?'

'Yes.'

As all journalists will realise, this is pretty spectacular considering the first ten to fifteen years of your career will see you earning a salary so measly you'll become an expert at cadging free drinks and raiding your parents' change pot for coins.

Or, in my case, being lucky enough to have a Mal who charged me pittance rent.

I was impressed. Rob was actually a grown-up man.

As the clock ticked towards 3am, I decided it was bedtime. Solo bedtime.

But then Rob said something which, while not romantic, was certainly true to his nation's straight, no-bullshit ethos: 'So, this is the point we figure out whether we are going to be mates, or something more. Are we going to kiss or what?'

I looked at him, and I remember this moment etched onto my memory as carefully and gently as if by a calligrapher's brush.

I got up.

I sat on his lap, with my legs tucked behind me. I placed my hands on his face and, as I came closer, I could feel his heart beating faster and faster – *badoombadoomBADOOM*.

And then we kissed.

It wasn't Roman candles or sparklers. This was far older than that. This was a spark that started in the centre of the earth; it surged through the ground, past rock and roots, and entered through our feet.

Perhaps it might have stopped there, as just a very good kiss. But every time Rob and I kissed, every day, for six years, it never once lost the spark that shot from a point beyond our understanding and wrapped us in its glow.

The reason I know that love like this wasn't delusion, or what we wanted to believe, is because I always recognise its counterpart in other people.

Like this video made by a colleague of mine who filmed her eighty-year-old grandfather talking about how much he loved his wife, who had dementia and lived in a home.

He presses her hand, strokes her hair. He looks at her with the desperation of someone who is trying to make smoke stand still and doesn't know how to stop pieces of her evaporating, as must happen every day.

At the end of the video, he says simply: 'I love her.'

And I feel it.

I feel the love he had for her and I recognise its counterpart in me, in terms of what I had for Rob. There are people I instantly see it in, and people I don't. Trying to contain Big Love from your voice is impossible; so if it isn't there, I don't think it ever was. If you're wondering if this is IT, it isn't.

Because real love is light, it is fire. It catches and blows into a million sparks and it settles down on you hot and sizzling, and when it cools, it becomes strength, it becomes part of you; it changes you entirely.

'So, there's something I should probably tell you,' said Rob.

We were in a taxi on the way to his house after dinner, around four weeks into dating. We held hands across the middle seat – gingerly, because there was a weird white stain exactly on the spot you'd expect a weird white stain to be.

Things had moved really quickly, but I knew I had never been happier.

Two weeks before, when I was still deciding whether to go on another date, I fell ill. I had a cough like a sailor who smoked forty unfiltered roll-ups a day, and everything in my chest hurt. I looked like two horror films that had had sex with each other – everything oozing, red eyes and a vacant stare from too much cough syrup.

I didn't want to see him. Even my mother tried to get off the phone as quickly as she could while I hacked into the receiver, and this is a woman who used to let me blow my nose on her nightie.

'I'm bringing you chicken noodle soup,' he said.

'Oh God, no. I just can't face seeing anyone.'

'That's okay, you don't have to. I'll leave it on the step, ring the doorbell and scoot away so you won't have to see me.'

I paused. 'You'd seriously do that?'

'Yes.'

'This isn't some kind of mind-fuck where the soup is a metaphor for something else?'

'No. It's real-life, no-strings-attached (mainly because I'll make sure I remove the string ha-ha) chicken noodle soup.'

He turned up with rapidly cooling soup in a giant pot. I let him in the door. 'You look beautiful,' he said, kissing me on the lips.

I caught a glimpse of my reflection. My hair was matted at the back. My nose was peeling. And looking back at him, I saw he was serious.

Who was this man, who made chicken noodle soup, and who was starting to move so fluidly through my life, through my bloodstream and into my heart, when I had no recollection of how I let him past the gate?

Winning my heart was not easy, yet he had passed every stage. He called, he genuinely listened to what I said. When I stayed over at his house for the first time, we didn't sleep together.

Instead, we kissed all night. In the morning, I woke up next to a steaming cup of tea with a ceramic zebra's head emerging from the liquid.

'Well done, fucko,' it seemed to say, 'you're a goner.'

A week later, our social calendars collided at his house, although we hadn't been due to meet. I had been at a bar for a friend's birthday; he had been out to a dinner party. The birthday shindig was full of pretentious twats in Camden, and I didn't think Rob would mind me turning up at his house. I texted, he texted, and it was on.

When I came through the front door, which was already open, Rob was cuddling Daisy while sprawled in a cream armchair.

'Hello,' he said, smiling with the flush of many red wines. 'We're going to get married and have brown babies. We're going to make International Beige babies. I love you.'

By a hair's breadth, I was more sober than he was. 'I'm sorry, what?'

I needed to make sure I'd heard what I heard. After a few drinks Rob's accent was even more incomprehensible so, phonetically, it sounded like: 'Harro. We'zxsplish married. Brown babies. Shminternational Beige. Ruvoo.'

He repeated himself, I listened. For the first time in my life, I wasn't scared. When men had declared their love before, and I wasn't ready or I didn't feel it, I would nod and plot my escape through gritted smiles.

But I could feel something huge shifting; tectonic plates of New Zealand and India moved across continents and lay beneath our feet, layered on top of one another.

'So, do you remember what I said yesterday?' he asked me the next morning, with his arm stretched underneath my pillow, breathing in the back of my neck as I faced another cup of tea with the floating zebra head. Clearly, he thought I liked this mug when in fact I felt it silently mocked me.

'Yes,' I replied, my smile hidden from view.

'And?'

I wriggled around under the sheets in a 180-degree turn to

face him and looked him in his blue eyes. 'You know I feel it. I just want to say it at the right time.'

He looked happy, his eyes meeting his smile. 'You're so beautiful.'

'Stop trying to get me to say it.'

A few months into our relationship, summer had finally arrived and we were in the park, lying next to each other.

Rob said: 'Haven't we somehow, through pure chance, got exactly the kind of love you can make a whole life out of? I never saw this coming but now I have you, I'll never let you go.'

I loved it so much I immediately wrote it down on a napkin.

I don't know how he knew.

'It's fair to say he was smitten from the start,' said Anoushka, a close friend of his.

At the beginning I'd tried to come up with excuses for why we shouldn't have another date, because deep down I didn't want to get attached and risk being hurt. But he always knew, and his faith gave me faith in myself, and in us.

When I felt myself falling, when I felt that parts of me were reforming into something new and different, and full of Rob, it terrified me. I had never been this happy, had never experienced this kind of connection, and I felt it rewriting the person I was, strand by strand.

I looked up from the crook of his arm where my head was resting and said: 'Rob, I'm so scared something bad is going to happen to us. I feel so happy but I feel like I don't deserve it, like it's too perfect.'

He kissed my head. 'Nothing's going to happen, honey.'

Sometimes we place so much pressure and expectation on love. It's as if it sits in a glass bottle on a high shelf, and we believe that if we take small sips of it, it will fix the problems we have in our lives. And when it doesn't, it feels like we failed.

The problem isn't whether or not we love. Or how strong it is, or even whether it's the right kind of love. The fact is, we are conditioned from an early age to believe that love is perfection – not just that it is a goal to strive for, but that it is a solution, a rescue from an otherwise unhappy existence.

I don't know a single person who doesn't want to be loved. Who doesn't want to hear the reassuring murmur of another person's breath in the room, to feel the counterpoint of yourself reflected in someone else and draw comfort from how well they know and love you.

But fairy tales and the dream sold by society that love and marriage are the main currencies with which to buy happiness do not prepare you for the challenges that lie ahead.

So when you are holding hands in a car, avoiding weird white stains, speeding to a future of fresh sheets, mugs of zebra tea and the legs of your loved one wrapped around you, and the person you are falling in love with says: 'So, there's something I should probably tell you,' you are already gone.

'Okay,' I replied, 'what's that? You're already married? You're gay? You want me to be your beard? You're not actually a nerd? I hate to tell you, but I think you're a pretty big nerd.'

I always was the talkative one in our relationship and usually my verbal diarrhoea made Rob smile.

But this time his smile didn't quite meet the crinkles around his eyes, and my words fell flat, oddly hollow in the space between us. Suddenly, that middle seat stretched into a desert and we were standing on opposite dunes trying to see each other under the night sky.

'It's not a big deal, but I'd rather I told you. We have depression running through my family, and I have it as well. I haven't been properly depressed for a long time, but I thought I should tell you.'

'Okay,' I said. 'I'm glad you told me.'

'There's nothing to worry about, okay?' he said.

'Okay.' I pressed his big, calloused hand tightly and kissed the back of it. I wasn't concerned; I didn't think any more of it. He might as well have told me he had athlete's foot.

A comfortable silence fell between us, and we watched the trees in the nearby woodland pass us by, the red lights of parked cars along the edge, its occupants creeping around for love in a dark place.

Depression wasn't something I knew much about.

I knew people felt sad, and had trouble getting out of bed, but then after a while they stopped feeling so terrible. I only knew of one friend who had it after undergoing surgery, and she recovered eventually. So how bad could it be?

Like the web of an unpleasant dream, I brushed it away from the corner of my mind. *If Rob wasn't worried, I wasn't worried. I trust him completely.*

I was happy and I had finally found the love of my life.

There is something unusual going on with the beech trees.

Whole forests of them cover the area of Fiordland in New Zealand, and these ones aren't like the golden glades you see in England, where writers dream up bunnies in waistcoats and Prince Charming trots through on a white horse.

On either side of our path, the trees are covered in lichen; dark green lace gobbling up entire trunks, curtains made of feathery fronds draped from branch to branch. The trees fan out deep into the distance, an immense tangle of roots appearing to climb into other worlds.

I have never seen anything like it.

We are forty-two walkers swallowed up in this vast, primordial sprawl along the Milford Track. Soon, the ethereal greenery surrounds us completely; it humbles us, renders us mute.

Although the landscape seems forgotten, a closer look reveals it is more like the earth dreamed up from a time before we messed her up. We have been given the chance to see our planet in her youth, and there is nothing eerie about her.

Not today, anyway.

She is reminding us of how the world was, how it still could be, which in turn makes us introspective and think about who we are, the things we've pointlessly been holding on to and who we want to be.

*We don't have the luxury of distracting ourselves from the bigger questions. Smartphones don't work here and it's hard holding a conversation when you're wheezing up a mountain.*

*Everything that loves water has gathered. In the distance, day-old waterfalls spray white foam from cracks in the rock face. Beneath my feet grow tiny intricate mosses, alive and springy, not like the decaying patches in half-remembered gardens back home.*

*I let the other walkers move past to allow a pocket of solitude, time to think and close my eyes. As they move on ahead, the sound of their walking poles clacking in the distance, my head has never felt so empty, so peaceful and free from worry.*

*This is right where I am meant to be.*

*I know people say that in romantic films when they are catching each other's lives by the tips of their fingers at a train station or an airport, but despite the fact that I am alone, dressed in walking gear that makes me look like a ten-year-old boy and starting to smell like a ripe sock, this is the place.*

*My expectations for life were left behind on the boat that dropped us off at the start of the track. I unpacked the burden of concern my friends and family have for me, the hope of having babies, the worry that I will be alone for the rest of my life, the hurt of the last few years, the loss of a world that once had a husband, a dog and a house in it.*

*Here, it's just me and Rob.*

*Coming to New Zealand, I hoped, would reset some of the terrible events of last year. While in Auckland, Rob took his own life in the woods at a nature reserve.*

*Thinking about his last moments set off a primal growl with grief in its throat; it smells of earth, sadness, tears and love; it sounds like hearts cracking, lives breaking and reforming.*

*When it comes to suicide, every pinprick of light that surrounded the darkness of their death is pounced upon; we hope against hope that our loved ones, while they died alone, didn't just die with despair.*

*So the fact that my nature-loving husband killed himself in the woods tells me something of him was still in there before he died.*

*But the more I read into his death, the more I feel as if only now am I beginning to understand Rob. Many people assumed I came here to find out why he died. But I came to find out how he became the man I loved when he lived.*

# Chapter Two

Rob didn't live that far from us – about five minutes by car – but it may as well have been on a different planet. Balham was all yummy mummies and cute delis.

Streatham, where Rob lived, was chicken-shop-land. Pavements littered with tiny bones, home to people who drifted like lost ghosts along the high street vomiting strong, stale beer in dusty doorways, shop fronts selling mobile phone covers and protein powder.

The area did have some fabulous houses, though; grand Victorian beauties with frilly crenulations, dark-red brick and white piping around the edges. Houses with gardens – a rarity in London – and big, open greens where people walked their dogs and paused under huge, leafy trees for shade.

The first time I took a taxi to his house, his instructions were: 'Go down Oakdale Road, you'll see a row of Victorian houses. When you come to the oddly shaped 1970s butt-ugly triangle house, that's mine.'

The house was as grim as he described it; rebuilt after being bombed during the war and badly made, with thin walls and low ceilings. The bathroom looked like it was being eaten slowly by mould, and the kitchen counter was buckling under moisture.

It was a brown, school dinner of a building. But Rob loved it – it was his first house, and I respected that.

Rob owned it with his friend Mikey, who lived there along with another friend, Rob Cruise. It had a particular feel and smell to it that places inhabited only by men do – half-wolf, half-human.

It was reasonably tidy, but smears of mud and blood on the walls revealed its true nature as a den, and I knew there were parts of the house that probably hadn't been cleaned since they moved in.

There was a fish tank. Not the pretty tropical kind with guppies and angelfish. This one housed two ugly-as-sin axolotls: prehistoric-looking salamanders, one pure white, the other a boggy green.

I couldn't get rid of them – it would have been like a stepmother sending the kids to boarding school. But luckily the bog green one was slowly nibbling the white one to death (they can regenerate their limbs but evidently not quickly enough when someone is using you as a regular snack), so there would be a resolution either way without my interference.

With Rob's dog Daisy in the mix – then a hazelnut-coloured, feisty one-year-old who did not initially approve of my entry into his life – I had to adjust to dog hair, bits of chewed-up toys she liked to squirrel away under her bed, and muddy paw prints tattooed across the floor just after I cleaned it.

Daisy and I met on our third date.

I heard her long before I saw her, and it's a small miracle I didn't wet myself in fear – her bark sounded like it was piped through the lungs of a bear. I'd already seen her mugshot: big beautiful eyes, a tiny pink star on her nose and a terrifying jaw that revealed her pit bull genes – and, as I stood outside Rob's front door, I imagined those very same jaws clamping around my bottom.

'I made sure I walked her for two hours so she won't drive us crazy on our date,' texted Rob a few hours before.

Rob's ex-girlfriend Monique had bought Daisy as a Christmas present, and when puppy met man it was love at first sight. As my experience of pets was limited to goldfish and an ill-fated stint with a kitten that didn't last long, I couldn't quite understand that bond between a dog and its human. But in Rob and Daisy, you saw how much they were knitted into each other.

They'd spend hours on the floor cuddled together, arm in arm, Daisy's paws in utter submission, Rob rubbing her belly, murmuring: 'Who's my little girl, hmm?' Sometimes, it was pretty galling – when Rob was withdrawn or feeling particularly low – that the dog got more love than I did.

In fact, my cousin Prarthana actually said to him once: 'When I met you, I wasn't sure I liked you. You seemed to pay more attention to your dog than you did to Poorna.' (Needless to say, this was after it was established that she liked him.)

There is no doubt, however, that animals help people with depression, partly because they supply companionship and unconditional love, and also because they provide a purpose. Rob took his care of Daisy seriously – which meant that, as a big dog, she needed regular walking, and that got him out of the house even when he didn't feel like it.

On our date, however, there were no cuddles for Daisy, and she looked outraged that another woman was sitting next to His Lordship. Every time we laughed or tried to come close, she'd get up off her bed, blow loudly through her nose and wiggle her big bottom over to us, trying to get some attention.

She tried these tactics every single time I visited Rob's house over the next eighteen months as a guest, and didn't deviate from her course even after he asked me to move in with him. Although she grew to love me, from time to time she'd rebel, picking a delight such as choosing to rub her muddy bum only on my side of the bed, or staging a dirty protest in my office.

On moving-in day, when I turned up on the doorstep with

lots of boxes, Daisy inspected everything as if to say, *Bitch, please.*

Rob was less attentive. He met me at the door and announced abruptly: 'I'm on deadline.' So I was left to unpack a lot of it on my own, and, over the next few days, I threw myself into spring-cleaning the entire house. I tidied up cans, bottles, packets of food; wiped the cupboards from top to bottom; ran an inventory of the sauces, pickles and jars lurking in the back of the fridge; washed our sheets in bleach to remove traces of Daisy-related mud; lifted everything up and swept, mopped and vacuumed.

While Rob worked in his office – also known as the converted garage – he kept the door closed. When I tried to pop in to talk to him, I found him hastily shutting a drawer.

'Ooh, is that a present for me?' I asked. I was waiting for him to make a big show of me moving in – I had hinted enough times that Mal had set a high standard. (She welcomed me with a Capri-Sun and my name spelled out in magnets on the fridge.)

'No, there's nothing for you in there,' he replied.

*Aw,* I thought, *he's trying to fob me off. I bet he has a surprise.*

The memory slid down a crack; I forgot that he never did give me anything.

\*

Soon after I moved in, Rob and I were sitting up in bed when he said: 'I don't want you to worry, but I'm going to talk to my GP about going on some mild antidepressants.'

I wasn't worried.

'Are you okay? Is there anything I can do?' I thought it was like going to get antibiotics. He'd have the medication, it would fix it. It made me think he was on top of it and being responsible about it too.

The year was 2010. This was before I knew anything substantial about depression. When I think of this person, the person I was, I am both envious of her naivety and sad because she had no idea what she was dealing with.

'I'm fine, honestly. I just think it's best to get on top of it before it gets worse.'

'Did something happen to, you know, cause it?'

'No, it just happens sometimes in cycles. It comes on and goes away again after a while.'

'What does it feel like?' I snuggled closer, trying to wrap my arms around his torso which sometimes seemed so broad it was like trying to encircle a huge tree.

'Think about your best day,' he said. 'Everything is going right for you. The sun is shining. It should be the happiest day of your life, right?

'Depression is feeling as if you are having the worst day of your life, over and over, even when you should be happy, like on the day your first child is born.

'How you *want* to feel doesn't make a difference because

*this* is how you feel. You are extremely sad and there is nothing you can do to escape it.'

There was a shiver in the room, as if something darker had been summoned in for show-and-tell, and now it was circling our bed, smacking its lips.

And then all of a sudden it was gone. I didn't give it a moment's thought.


In the first six months, Rob Cruise moved out and Mikey stayed.

Guests were a regular feature of our life, whether they were Kiwi relatives who'd come to stay for a few weeks or visitors for dinner. We'd eat in the lounge with its wooden floorboards and dodgy low ceiling, and, if the weather was warm, we'd sit out in the garden.

The garden was the most beautiful thing about the house. Rob showed me before and after pictures, and a lot of work had gone into digging a pond, creating little nooks for certain types of flowers, each pocket telling a story. Snake's-head fritillaries bowed their heads under larger shrubs, alliums stuck fluffy purple balls up as far as they could go. Plants with leaves like finest lace shared space with his loud and proud banana palm tree.

One day, we were visited by a friend who brought along a rescued Mediterranean spur-thighed tortoise named Aubrey.

Rob's eyes lit up. 'Oh my God. I've always wanted one.'

As it clomped around in the garden, it gave us the most evil stare I have seen on a creature. Like if you replaced the jackal that gave birth to Damien with a tortoise.

I was concerned about the growing ark of animals in our home. Along with Daisy, there were some newts, my (rapidly ailing) goldfish and the axolotls – who were increasingly in my bad books after I discovered the blood worms they ate were stored NEXT TO THE ICE TRAY in our freezer. But Aubrey was here to stay.

Despite Rob's devotion, Aubrey spent his entire time trying to head-butt or hump people's shoes. Daisy and I were united in that we hated him, and we were pleased when Aubrey – during his first attempt at emancipating himself from our house – finally disappeared.

'Oh well,' I shrugged, 'you gave it your best shot, Rob.'

Rob looked at me. 'What do you mean? I have to look for him.'

'Why? He was a total bastard that spent the entire time trying to attack our feet and he doesn't even like us very much.'

'He's my creature,' said Rob, on the verge of tears. 'He was in *my* care and I lost him. I *have* to find him.'

I was surprised by Rob's reaction, partly because I didn't see how anyone could love Aubrey, but mostly because I hadn't seen Rob this emotional in a while. For some time it had been hard to get a grip on how he felt, and when I asked him if he was all right, he'd say: 'I'm fine.' Even when we had company – guests he'd invited himself – he'd leave me to do all the talking and disappear for what seemed like hours.

Yet he spent half the night combing the garden with a head torch and eventually found Aubrey in the back alley where he had made a break for it, but had fallen asleep as the sun went down.

After a few more escape attempts, and similar search parties, the final straw came when Aubrey chose to sit at the bottom of our pond rather than remain in our garden a moment longer.

'I fished him out,' Rob said gloomily.

'That tortoise needs to go,' I replied.

Shortly after Aubrey left (donated to some mad-eyed tortoise lover who said to me: 'You must be so sad to let him go.' I replied: 'Devastated.'), Mikey also moved out.

My older sister Priya, returning from New York after splitting from her first husband, asked if she could stay with us for a while. Like Rob, she also worked successfully as a freelance science journalist.

We had a three-bedroom house, she was one of my favourite people, Rob was one of my favourite people – I was in heaven. They shared a love of science, and Priya found it easy and calm to be in our house. Her presence also distracted me from gradual changes I noticed in Rob's behaviour.

After moving in, the first thing I noticed was that he started spending ridiculous amounts of time in the bathroom. I didn't want to be some kind of weirdo who lurked outside, but when he was in there for bordering on thirty or forty minutes, I began to wonder whether he was prone to monster shits and had kept it secret from me this entire time.

'Rob, what on earth are you doing in there?'

'Jesus, woman, can't you just leave me in peace?'

You can see why I stopped bugging him when he was on the toilet. It's not cool to be the person who clock-watches another person's dump.

The second thing I noticed was his insomnia.

Rob smoked, and the first time I went round to his house for dinner, he puffed on a couple of cigarettes during the course of our evening. Towards the end, he rolled up a joint, which took me aback.

'No thanks,' I said, as he offered it to me. I didn't do drugs, and I was a bit surprised that Rob, being thirty-four then, hadn't quite grown out of smoking weed, a drug I associated with spotty teenagers. (Mainly because I tried it when I was a spotty teenager.)

After a bit more digging, I found out that Rob actually smoked weed every day. Sometimes in the morning, and definitely at night. I didn't know anyone who smoked daily, and

I didn't want to. I'd dated a couple of guys who had smoked dope when I was younger, but I felt deeply uncomfortable around Rob using it.

'I'm sorry, Rob,' I told him after several dates, 'but the drugs thing is a dealbreaker. I understand if that's what you want to do with your life, but I can't be with someone who uses that every day. I don't think it's right.'

We had a long chat about it.

'How is smoking weed different to drinking?' he asked.

'It's two different highs – I'm bouncing all over the place while you're in slow motion. It takes you about five minutes to laugh at a joke I've made. Plus I can get mine at a corner shop; you have to call your grim drug dealer.'

'I think it's semantics but . . . '

'It's not semantics, it's the fucking law.'

He used drugs recreationally and had friends who did the same, but it was no big deal, he said. 'To be honest, I've been cutting it out of my life anyway, so if this doesn't work for you, then that's fine.'

'It doesn't work for me,' I said.

The first year of our relationship was blissful, but this was the one dark spot. A spot that kept recurring.

I'd find out he'd gone dog walking with a friend and had a bit of his weed. Or we'd go to a party and he'd spend most of the evening tripping from one joint to another, the miasma and fug gripping him in place.

'I didn't realise you wanted me to quit completely,' he said when I told him how unhappy it made me. 'But it's no big deal, I'll give it up.'

So he gave it up. I didn't see a trace of it in our home, and that's when his insomnia began.

Where we once went to bed together and woke up in each other's arms, I would often go to bed alone, his side dark and cold. 'I'm sorry, honey,' he'd say, 'I just can't get to sleep.'

When he did sleep, he had nightmares that made him yell out. From the research I did, I understood that the insomnia was part of depression, but the weed had probably dampened his ability to dream for however long he had been smoking, as it has been shown to suppress REM sleep and all the important functions it performs.[1] Now that he was starting to dream again, maybe the nightmares that had been held at bay for so long were lining up to be heard.

I hated that we didn't go to bed at the same time. I felt that we were no longer like two walruses who fell asleep with our flippers wrapped around each other and were more like anglerfish going it alone with the light snuffed out.

The longer it went on, the more I felt the insomnia take shape. It pooled around our lives and slid blocks of ice between us.

As it began to claim him, it robbed us of breakfasts together, drew lines under his eyes and laughed when we made plans. 'You'll never end up doing them,' it said. 'I'll make sure he's too tired to even get out of bed.'

I also became concerned about whether he was getting

out of bed in the morning to work. This resulted in guerrilla tactics and using Priya as my eyes on the inside. I'd call from the office and ask: 'So, how's work? How are you? Anyway, quick question – is Rob awake?'

'Um, freelancers' code, sis,' she replied. Meaning, it was up to freelancers how they divided their day, so she wasn't going to tell.

'He's asleep, isn't he?'

'I can neither confirm nor deny.'

While Priya lived with us, I didn't feel the full impact of Rob's changing behaviour. Instead of watching TV with him, I watched it with her. We went to films together, cooked big dinners at home and went out for drinks.

The loneliness only set in after Priya left. I didn't even notice that we hadn't actually lived on our own together during the whole two and a half years we had known each other.

I didn't tell a lot of people Rob had depression. When we increasingly began to cancel on double dates, dinner parties and visits to art galleries – embarrassingly, sometimes a matter of hours before we were due to attend because Rob would only decide he couldn't go at the very last minute – I didn't know how to talk to people about it. Partly because I didn't want people to feel sorry for me, or for them to view Rob differently, and partly because he himself found it hard to say: 'I feel unwell because I'm depressed.' It was always the flu, insomnia or a bad stomach.

When you or your loved ones don't have a mental illness, it is almost impossible to comprehend what it's really like. It's not black and white; in fact, it deals almost exclusively in grey.

Of course, I started to feel alone a lot. There was just stuff I thought couples did, like go to garden centres together, fight over IKEA furniture and have coffee. Silly, boring, mundane things, but their absence keenly felt when you don't have them.

But life with Rob wasn't predictable. One moment I would be confused and hurt by his coldness, the next I would have my beloved back. Bunches of fat, yellow daffodils would sit as quiet declarations of love by my bedside table, kisses were shared in the hallway, elaborate dinners of slow-cooked ribs would be laid at the table. And no matter how bad our day or how low he felt, we began and ended with *I love you*.

The truth was that although there were a lot of times when I was on my own, and I couldn't understand why Rob was in bed so much, there was love and there was goodness.

We held our little world safe behind closed doors, and I didn't want other people's judgements placed upon us. The overwhelming attitude towards depression is acknowledged in the summary of the illness on the NHS website:

'Some people still think that depression is trivial and not

a genuine health condition. They're wrong. Depression is a real illness with real symptoms, and it's not a sign of weakness or something you can "snap out of" by "pulling yourself together".'

Although I didn't fully understand what it was, I Googled 'how to help your partner when they have depression'.

During my explorations, I found a superb blog by author Jamie Flexman, who argued that it is actually a physical illness, not a mental one, because it is caused by the brain.

'Last I heard,' he says, 'the brain [is] a part of the body, and a damn important one at that.'

His description of what depression actually feels like also helped.

'Depression is like trying to run through water and being told to get over it is akin to suddenly being able to move like you can on dry land. It's impossible. You can grit your teeth and attempt to get some momentum going but ultimately the density will prevent you from moving quickly.

'When depression has its grip on you, life becomes water. The air around you becomes water, crushing you with its weight, and even the simplest tasks become difficult. You feel sluggish, both mentally and physically, and nothing can snap you out of it.

'You have essentially become trapped inside your own prison and true access to your brain lies behind that locked door. Sometimes, briefly, you are allowed outside to stretch your legs but you know this is temporary. Eventually you will have to return to your cell and wait patiently for a time when you are given another opportunity to function like a normal member of society.'[2]

I only learned what depression was like after going through it after Rob died, and even then it wasn't the same type of depression. Mine was a natural response to a life event, in this case a bereavement. His was a lifelong, clinical condition.

It filled me with horror that he suffered like this for so much of his life. I was also filled with admiration for what he still managed to achieve, despite feeling the way he did. He helped so many people, but for someone so open and giving to others, he was an enigma when it came to his own feelings.

When he hadn't slept for a while, or when he was having a bad depressive time, he was unable to communicate what was going on in his head. 'I'm fine, honestly, honey,' came the refrain.

Having never suffered from depression at that time, and still being that naive idiot who took things at face value, I believed he was fine. Of course he wasn't fine.

He took great pains to maintain the appearance of the life he wanted. The one in which he didn't have depression, where he could be a good, stable partner and one day a father.

He couldn't talk to me about it because telling me meant that he'd have to acknowledge that *this* was his life, not the life he sketched out for himself with me and our babies by his side.

The cost to him on a daily basis must have been immense.

Dealing with depression while trying to work and be part of a relationship, which included making dinner, pitching in with housework and trying to see friends – I don't know how he did it.

In fact, thinking about it now, the cost of striving for normality for him was absolute. He held on to that dream so tightly that there was nothing but for it to shatter.

*I am in Te Ngaere Bay, a remote place in the north, with Rob's*
*aunts, now mine, Felicity and Gabrielle.*

*Traditionally, I don't like swimming in the sea.*

*As my family originally come from Mangalore in South India,*
*a necklace of land along the Arabian Sea, home to coconut trees*
*and fat, slippery mackerel cooked in tamarind, where fishermen*
*slip in and out of the water as easily as their fishing nets, this*
*makes me somewhat of a race traitor.*

*I don't like the cloying texture of the salt water on your skin*
*long after you have left it, sticky and needy, smelling like crea-*
*tures made of bone and gills, attracting flies to the silver salty*
*trails it leaves behind like an unwanted gift.*

*In New Zealand, though, the sea feels like a pure thing.*

*The bay is a sliver of golden beach, one side hemmed in by*
*jet-black rocks and a little outcrop that is accessible when the*
*tide is low. We clamber over to see a rusted winch (we wonder if*
*it's for whaling) and, over the ridge, seaweed is spread out like*
*a pale red crepe carpet.*

*At the other end of the beach is a much rougher part of*
*sea. Waves crash relentlessly against the rock; there is even a*
*pohutukawa tree growing from the tip of one craggy peak.*

*In the evening light, from the veranda of our rented house, we*
*squint our eyes against the sun. Although the bay is protected by*

a reef, it is having trouble fending off the waves left behind by a cyclone passing through the Pacific.

As the waves gather and beat the drum before sunset, they shoot up spray that rises above the rock and towards the hilly green ridge hemming in the bay. The shore grows molten and, below the tips of pine trees lining the ridge, the deep folds of mountains in the distance and the grass lining the dunes, the water turns silver.

In the evenings, dotterels pass through, as if they were on skateboards, sailing serenely down the shoreline. In the daytime, kingfishers – a bird, like hornbills, owls and nightjars, that Rob and I felt were part of our shorthand as a couple – zip from one tree to another, holding something tasty in their beaks.

We also see seagulls – which I regard as donkeys of the ocean – pluck hapless clams from the beach and drop them from a great height until their soft white belly is exposed for the pecking.

The Pacific is not as cold as the North Sea, but it is definitely colder than the Caribbean. I spend the first day in Te Ngaere dipping my toes in, screaming like a character in a pantomime and running back to the safety of the sundeck.

By the second day, it's raining, but I want to kayak despite the water still looking a bit choppy. As I drag the boat to the water, I realise, as wave after wave hits me, that I am not going to be able to get this thing in or, indeed, even steer it back. I feel the tug of the sea and it is saying, I am older and stronger than you, little girl, try it if you think you're hard enough.

I look back at the house and Felicity is half-laughing at

*my antics, and half-concerned the sea is going to swallow me whole.*

*So I decide to go for a swim. I have never gone for a swim when it is raining, and the water is far from warm, but I'm already wet.*

*I feel the round discs of clams beneath my feet, shuffling like cards, digging deep into the sand. The surf pounds against me, like a lover trying to close the door in my face,* Not today, not today.

*I kneel down in the sea, the cold water travelling up to my chest, the rain a soft pitter-patter from the sky, and I close my eyes.*

*I feel the spray, the scent of water and earth in my nose, the smell carrying the thoughts of an ocean, the shells of sea creatures crunching beneath my knees, the heartbeat of surf that pumps and swells against my body. It is like a dance I can never match, that moves far too elegantly for my feet. And then I remember: the sea moves. It shifts constantly, changes; it is never the same thing for more than one moment.*

*And this is what the land tries to make us forget. The land makes us think we are fixed, that all that happens to us is all we will ever be, that we are in control of our lives. It makes us believe that if you stay in one fixed place, you can be in charge of it all, you can be safe.*

*But it is a lie, utterly.*

# Chapter Three

I was never the type of girl who dreamed about weddings.

Perhaps that was because Indian weddings are horrendously long, the music sounds like bagpipes played by drunk people and there are thousands of guests. By the end of it, the bride and groom look like the propped-up corpse from *Weekend at Bernie's* because they have to stand on a stage the entire night and wait as each and every one of those people go up to congratulate them.

They also have to shake hands with the more enthusiastic guests – some of whom I've personally seen scratch their bums/pick their nose/not wash their hands after using the loo – and, no, the couple are not allowed to use hand sanitiser or wear disposable gloves.

It's even harder for the bride because along the way some masochist decided that not only was she going to have to don an extra-heavy sari or a lengha (a skirt and top that can weigh up to sixteen kilos), but the amount of gold she wears is only deemed sufficient when her spine curves like a coat hanger.

However, although Indian weddings are boring, the highlight is the food.

None of your insipid salmon en croûte shit or shoe-leather roast lamb – Indian food is superb at weddings because the longer it sits, the more flavoursome it becomes. And because caterers rely so heavily on word of mouth, and that mouth tends to be a collective of extremely critical aunts, any business serving bad food wouldn't last a minute.

But guess what? The bride and groom are lucky if they even get a sniff of it. They have to shake all those goddamn hands before they can even touch a plate, and Indians are notoriously good at honing in on all the best pieces of meat.

So, at around 1am, the bride and groom end up with a plate of prison food: yellowing rice and some gravy.

Thanks but no thanks.

Aside from the wedding ceremony, I also couldn't comprehend meeting someone I wanted to spend the rest of my life with.

Which wasn't to say that I didn't believe in romance, but while I had found myself dreaming about what my soulmate would be like, I'd never done the same with a husband. In the case of the former, I knew how I wanted to *feel* – which was safe, loved, like I was the centre of the other person's world. That they would make me laugh even when I felt grumpy and that I would never get sick of their company. Humming along the same wavelength.

But a *husband* is a completely different proposition. Choosing a husband or a wife requires practicality of a specific kind.

It doesn't matter if they like Taylor Swift and you like techno, or they like reality TV and you like Nordic noir. (But, hey – at least you'll have one thing in common: both your music tastes are terrible.) Unless you met at high school or university, you are likely to have a diverse range of interests and, guess what, none of that matters.

What matters is the big stuff. Do you want the same things from life? Do you share some of the same values? If one of you wants kids and the other definitely doesn't, or if one of you really wants to get married and the other doesn't believe in marriage, just shake hands, say thanks for coming, and walk away. You'll be saving yourself from a lot of repressed angst and stomach ulcers.

The reason why I didn't dream of a husband was because I didn't believe a man like Rob was possible.

During my twenties, I predominantly dated Asian men – by that I mean from the Indian subcontinent, which includes India, Pakistan, Bangladesh and Sri Lanka. I just assumed I would end up marrying someone from my own culture because things like family, duty and a mutual desire to have kids was just easier when someone already knew what the deal was.

Like not having to explain to someone what a bucket bath was. This may not sound like the stuff of fairy tales, but it was about comfortableness and not having to deal with someone saying, 'Ew! You people have a bath out of a *bucket*?'

For the record, this happens mainly in India where showers and bathtubs are extremely wasteful because water is such a precious commodity. When you're bathing out of a bucket using a beaker, you become a lot more attuned to how much water you actually need. You also save money on a bathroom radio as you won't be in there long enough to squeeze out even half a Taylor Swift song.

I'm not saying I ever wrote: 'Dear Diary, when will I meet my prince who understands bucket baths? Sigh ... ' But I think I unconsciously veered towards men from a similar background, which didn't make sense because my parents, and extended family for that matter, are pretty liberal. Unlike a lot of other British Asian parents – some of whom go loco if their daughter or son so much as looks at someone from a different caste, let alone a different country – they didn't really care about that sort of thing.

'The most important thing,' my parents frequently said, 'is that we want you to be happy.'

For someone who didn't think she'd ever get married, when I did get engaged I spent terrible sums of money on stuffed parrots from Paperchase, went on endless Etsy searches to find bird-themed stationery and cocktail sticks. My fiancé liked birds and he'd get birds.

Rob observed this with amused detachment.

'Do you think the bird thing might be getting out of hand?' he said, lifting one of the clay bird Christmas decorations I'd bought from the local garden centre, while I was furiously gluing bird wallpaper to a tin can.

'You're the one who likes birds, remember!'

'Yes, I like bird-watching. As in live birds.' He mimed flapping motions. 'This is starting to look like the collection of crazy people obsessed with unicorns or porcelain piglets.'

'Get out.'

A few months before, Rob and I had flown to Malaysia, with conversations about getting married tucked away neatly alongside our passports. I knew he was going to propose at some point, and that the ring was somewhere on his person, but I just didn't know exactly where or when.

I waited a couple of days but there were no obvious signs. Then he suggested going bird-watching. He had tried to coax me on bird missions around England, but I'd always refused on account of it being cold and muddy.

Malaysia was different – it was our favourite kind of weather, hot and humid. At night we lay under a fan, curled into each other's bodies, and the day was spent in shorts while drinking cold beer.

After a couple of days of this, we visited Gunung Raya, the highest mountain in Langkawi, which was home to hornbills, one of his favourite birds.

The mountain rose above dense, green rainforest, peaks

covered in a tight carpet of trees that spread into mist at the furthest reaches of our eyeline. As we drove up, Rob periodically stopped the car, and we'd get out to watch and be still. He took out the binoculars I bought him for Christmas and peered into the distance.

Birdcall sounded, their final words of the day echoing around the mountain range as sunset drew in. No hornbills: we dejectedly headed back to the car.

Then across a dip in the forest valley, we saw an entire flock of them flying over sedately, their huge wings cutting through the warm, soupy air, their beaks a distinct shape against a dark pink sky. We stood in silence, enrapt, holding hands and needing no words to say how beautiful it was, how lucky we felt.

That would have been a perfect moment to propose, wouldn't it? But no such luck.

A couple of days later, we went to Telaga Tujuh, or Seven Wells, a place of milky waterfalls and views of the sea, an aquamarine shimmer in the distance. This was less romantic than it sounds. On the way there, Rob kept stopping the car to bird-watch, and then we had a steep climb to the top, which involved sweating heavily. That's why I look like I'm having a stroke in most of my engagement photos.

When I finally got to the top and passed out under a tree, he said: 'Come here, I want to show you this new bird I've spotted.'

'NO. No more. I don't give a shit about birds. Take your birds and fuck off.'

But he insisted and by the time I grumpily hobbled to the edge of the waterfall, wiping beads of sweat from my forehead, he got down on one knee.

'Would you do me the honour of being my wife?'

On the walk down, I couldn't stop looking at my ring, a teardrop diamond. He kept saying the word fiancée with a huge smile on his face. Then, as an odd seal of approval as we got in the car, we saw a hornbill perched on top of a tree nearby.

That night, we spent the whole evening drinking beer with our feet dug in the sand of our beachside bar and sketched out our wedding plans.

'Are you sure you don't want to have a Catholic ceremony?' I asked, partly because we would have to have a Hindu ceremony and partly because I was angling for another wedding dress.

He scoffed at the idea. 'No way,' he said.

'But your parents? Won't they want you to have one?'

He shook his head.

My family may have been liberal, but I knew that a Hindu ceremony was definitely going to happen. It wasn't that they insisted on it, but having grown up around these ceremonies, I wanted one even if it was more cultural than religious.

Who really knew whether walking around the fire seven times bound you to seven lifetimes? It was the smell of fire and ghee, the red sari against brown skin and a long line of clinking bangles, eyes outlined in kohl and blessed sweets on the tongue, that made it a ceremony that bonded two people in marriage.

Rob's unquestioning acceptance of this was yet another reason why I knew he was the right man. Because to my family, it didn't matter that I was marrying a white man (who had a tattoo on the back of his head); what mattered was that he respected our family and culture.

Their initial concern was that he'd try to use white man's voodoo to lure me away from the holy bastions of Indianness – curry, bucket baths and familial duty – but they didn't prepare themselves for his zealous cultural uptake.

When they saw Rob attempt to eat with his hands, although he didn't quite get the technique right – you're supposed to use the tips of your fingers to eat the food, not smear it all over your hand like a glove – they appreciated the effort. When he wore a lungi – that's our version of the sarong – around the house teamed up with a Ramones t-shirt, they were stunned. While my mother bragged about it to our relatives, I lived in constant fear that the lungi would fall down – which it did once, ending up around his ankles as he was washing the dishes.

But, above all, Rob had a very strong sense of family and duty. We spoke at length about the family we wanted to create. We both had similar ideas of respect. He would offer to help Mum and Dad with the chores when we went over to visit. Unfailingly, he would take part in my mother's garden tour, where she would walk around like a conservationist at

Kew, showing us which plants were new, which were bloom-ing, which needed to be pruned. He was utterly engrossed in what she was saying, while I made fake snoring noises as I trailed behind.

Although I made fun of his local gardening harem, which consisted of a bunch of women in their sixties and seventies, he felt it was important to maintain a link with the older generation. 'It's important for me to have that,' he said – also referring to his male bird-watching friends – 'because my family, especially the older people in my life, are thousands of miles away.'

What I found difficult to reconcile was how he had such a strong sense of family, yet had spent nearly fifteen years living outside of New Zealand. The distance and cost of travelling alone meant he had seen his parents a handful of times in that period. My parents got needy if I didn't see them for three weeks, let alone three years.

I assumed the same would be true of him and, in fact, thought that a Catholic ceremony would be a nice way of honouring his parents and their faith. And did I mention I would get a second wedding dress?

But his lips drew thin when I pressed the matter. I didn't bring it up again, sensing bigger, deeper things swimming inside of him, unwilling to rise to the surface.

# Chapter Four

If we unravelled ourselves, unpacked every strand of DNA that makes us the human beings we are, it would unfurl a ladder to the sun and back. Our physical matter could stretch to other parts of the solar system, yet here we are, condensed and tightly packed into one tiny body.

We are arranged in so many different ways that not one of us is the same. Our brains are capable of thinking similar thoughts, but no two brains are identical. We are shaped by so many different things, from dealing with something as huge as death to the first ice cream we enjoyed on a summer's day.

Yet despite this, despite our individualities and the thousands of things that happen to us, the many nuances that make you the only *you* to have ever existed, we believe that illnesses of the brain can all be treated in the same way. And, even more damaging, that there is such a thing as a 'fix'.

The idea that we can fix mental illness (which, of course, implies you must be broken if you are suffering) is one that muzzles those who have it, and perpetuates a lot of stigma and myth for those who don't have it.

An illness such as depression affects about 20 per cent of people in the world, yet, as Professor Mark Williams of Oxford University, one of the most articulate and empathetic authorities on clinical psychology, would say, people think they know how heavy it is, and they don't know at all.

'None of us think we know the cure for cancer,' he said, 'but we all think we know the cure for depression.'

When Rob told me he was depressed, I genuinely thought it would be fixed. He mentioned antidepressants, and I assumed that at the end of it, he would be fine and back to normal.

To some people, 20 per cent may not sound like a lot, but that's one-fifth of the world's population. And for anyone with long-term depression, as Rob had, it recurs every year and to such a debilitating degree that it can last for up to four months. So the scale of it, says Prof. Williams, is much bigger than we think.

The US has the highest rates of depression; in the UK, one in four people will have a mental illness at some point. But when you view these statistics in light of how many people there are who feel they cannot talk about their depression, the numbers just don't add up. There must be so many people like

Rob, who can't admit to having depression and openly talk about it. There must be so many people like me, who don't always get it right.

If we had lived in a world which valued honesty around mental illness, perhaps Rob could have spoken about it. And perhaps I would have been able to listen.

Rob and I had been married a year. During the first three years of our relationship, I worked as a travel journalist, which meant some pretty amazing holidays and nights in hotels we could never afford in real life.

We visited Zanzibar and ate seafood suppers on beaches of white sand. We stayed in the best hotels in Malaysia when he proposed. On our first weekend break to Rome we had an actual, real-life butler named Maurice.

'He creeps me out,' I said.

'Well, you don't have to go on a date with him,' he replied.

I was sure Maurice was giving us a 'I know you scumbags can't actually afford this room, so I'm going to secretly take a shit in your toilet while you're out' look.

I can't imagine what other guests at these hotels thought, they with their trust funds and Rob striding across the resort, tattoos, skinhead and book in hand, but somehow he always managed to make friends wherever he went. From the middle-aged Austrian couple who smoked clove cigarettes in Bali, to the Australian couple we had dinner with in

Malaysia, he would be nattering away by the time I joined him after a run.

He was unapologetically friendly in that regard, and he'd say hello to people even if they didn't say it back, and had no qualms about age, race or craziness. It was a long-held belief that his ability to connect with people (and inspire us to do the same) was one of his most admirable traits.

Wesley, one of his oldest friends from New Zealand, summed it up best when he described how he met Rob.

'I met Rob (the only person I have ever known to have his name be an acronym for his full name, Robert Owen Bell) a long time ago at a party held at Louise Russell's place. We were fifteen.

'He walked right up to me, long hair, trench coat, a Ramones t-shirt and cargo shorts, looking just like Eddie Vedder. He thrust out his hand and said: "Hey, mate, I'm Rob. What's your name?" I answered Wes, to which he replied: "All right, Wes, how you doing?"

'We instantly became friends and over the years I saw him do that same thing countless times, the last of which was a 69-year-old lady who was missing most of her teeth by the name of Susan at the Riverhead Tavern. This was one week before he died.

'It didn't matter what she looked like, where she came from or where she was going; within minutes he had turned a complete stranger into another friend, another in a long list of friends.'

Although I can't say I was always happy to be presented with one of Rob's new 'friends' (one guy looked like he broke people's fingers for a living), holidaying was one of my favourite ways to spend time with him, not least because there was no chance of Daisy wriggling her way in, but also because we loved doing the same things: eating new and strange food, reading, napping and going on the occasional nature trip.

But it was on these early holidays as newlyweds that I started to notice the highs and lows that resulted from Rob's depression.

Our holiday to Portugal marked the first notable change. We spent the first two nights in Lisbon at a restored mansion set right by the castle, and planned to stay in a rural eco house near Sintra in the countryside, about an hour's drive away, for the rest of the week.

The first day, Rob couldn't get out of bed. It was as if he had been stapled to the sheets, his face drawn and pale, his stomach churning.

'Honestly, honey,' he said, 'I just need a day in bed and I'll be fine.'

I went down the stone steps to a little courtyard to have breakfast, and as I sipped orange juice, I mapped out my day. When I travelled solo I was used to exploring by myself, so this would be no different, I told myself.

Except at dinner, Rob still wasn't well. By day two, he managed to join me for breakfast and a bit of sightseeing. By day three, we hopped in our hire car and drove to the cottage we'd rented by the sea.

For most of the trip, Rob wasn't feeling great and was monosyllabic. The whitewashed cottage, though beautiful, with stained-glass windows, started to feel like a prison. It was freezing at night unless you sat right near the wood-burning stove and the sofa was only big enough to accommodate one person. Gunther, the German landlord, had also very considerately only paid for German cable TV.

In the middle of this stunning nature reserve with its wild grasses and clear, blue sea, I felt so miserable. On the fifth day of showering in cold water because the solar panel heating was busted, I just put my head in my hands and cried. I had never wanted to be home as much as I did at that moment.

And I couldn't turn to Rob for comfort because there was none. He was like an Easter egg with a smile painted on. I could tell he was there in person but there was nothing forthcoming from within.

'I'm sorry, honey,' is all he kept saying.

'It's all right, it's not your fault,' I kept saying.

I knew something was deeply wrong, so I Googled depression symptoms. Lack of energy, appetite changes, loss of interest in activities, insomnia. Again, I shelved my worries and set about trying to be cheery for Rob.

When we flew to Sicily a few months later, we rented an amazing villa; burnt orange walls flanked by glossy green trees and a pool in the back. I couldn't wait to spend the week with Rob, zip around in our car and go wine tasting, buy fresh fruit from the market and wind our limbs around each other for afternoon naps.

'We'll have to get up early,' I mused in the car journey to the villa as I flicked through our *Time Out* guide. 'Apparently the market closes at twelve.'

'Sure thing,' he replied.

At 9am, I bounced out of bed like Tigger. 'Can we go?' I asked.

'I didn't sleep well, honey,' came the reply. 'Can I just have a moment longer? Half an hour tops?'

I waited. And I waited. And every time, I was told: 'Half an hour longer, I promise.'

By now it was nearly twelve, and I was upset. I couldn't get in the car because only Rob had insurance, and although we had some loaves of bread in the villa left to us by the caretaker, we needed to do a proper shop.

'I'm sorry, I just don't feel well,' he said.

Again. I kept quiet and said: 'Okay, don't worry, we can go tomorrow. Just take it easy.' I tucked my needs behind his, but I wished he had told me instead of making me wait like a child who every half an hour asked: 'Can we go yet? Can we go yet?'

This would become an established pattern. Rob, unwilling to acknowledge that he wasn't physically capable of doing what it was that he had promised to do, drawing it out until the last minute, until I broke.

We went out for dinner because we didn't have any food in the house. There we were, at an open-air restaurant, the sea breeze lifting like ribbons and running through our hair. Other couples were leaning in closer, murmuring to each other, but he was bent over, barely touching his food.

'I'm sorry, it's just my stomach.'

Again.

I Googled 'insomnia stomach cramps' and, sure enough, chronic insomnia could cause stomach pain if the underlying cause was depression or anxiety.

The next day, the same thing happened. And I snapped. 'Rob, there is no food in the house. You promised we would go to the supermarket. I feel utterly trapped here – I can't leave because I'm not insured on the car!'

He eventually got up and we went to the market, spent time picking vegetables and looking at fresh fish, the morning almost forgotten. I cooked dinner and served it up with a great flourish.

But the evening was yet again like dining with a ghost.

'I'm sorry, I feel like I'm ruining your life,' he said.

'Of course you aren't,' I replied. 'But please, let's try to do something, go out and enjoy ourselves. This feels awful – like I'm just hanging around for you to wake up.'

I don't know what happened overnight, but the next day he was up. Sitting outside on a rattan chair, smoking a cigarette, squinting at the sun and drinking coffee.

We drank wine in Marsala. Two bicycles sat outside the

villa, so we hopped on them but after five minutes the strong sun humiliated us into turning back. We experimented with shaving his beard into mutton chops.

By the time we finished our last meal of the trip, at a restaurant called Da Vittorio by the sea, him in white linen, me in a yellow silk dress and sapphires from our wedding day, I had completely forgotten our inauspicious start. The sun was setting, casting us in gold, over a scene of white tablecloths and glasses of fizzy wine.

'We've got to come back here in a couple of years,' he said. 'It's perfect.'

I smiled, and felt our life coming back to us.

The remains of a perfectly cooked sea bass sat in front of us, and it seemed like this was all that had ever been, and ever would be.

When you're dealing with a loved one who has depression, it can be hard to know how to behave and what to say.

You know it's an illness, but that doesn't alleviate your loneliness any more than it alleviates their loneliness when you say: 'Hey, I'm here for you and you can talk to me about anything.'

Your emotions aren't allowed space. There is resentment but you can't focus it on them, because you realise that, as frustrating as it is for you, they are going through something far worse. But that doesn't mean your emotions don't exist.

There is anger, very raw and real anger, that you're dealing with a lot of it on your own, that you have to ask a stranger to get a bottle from the top shelf in Tesco because your own tall person is back home lying prone on a bed.

And at the same time you're not allowed to express that anger, not to your friends and family because you don't want them to feel sorry for you, and definitely not to your loved one because it's not their fault this is happening.

When you don't have depression, and you see them in bed, or unable to get up, you want to say: 'Get up! Go for a walk! Come with me to the gym!' because you think they'd feel better if only they could push themselves a bit harder. Even if you think you don't think it, there's a part of you that does.

I would not go onto a cancer ward and shout this out to patients who are recovering, so why did I expect it to work with Rob?

'Honey, are you sure you wouldn't feel better coming out with me for a bit?' I'd ask hopefully.

I kept asking. Did he want to walk Daisy? Did he want to get out of bed? Was he sure he didn't want to go to the cinema or out for dinner?

I mean, was I complicit in the bollocks attitude towards depression that maintained if he just got moving he'd feel better? Of course I was.

Sure, I did the shop (mostly) uncomplainingly. I washed the sheets, I cleaned our house, I represented us both at events. When he couldn't leave the house, I cooked huge dinners for him – goat curries swirling in tomato sauce, vinegary pork cooked with garlic, chicken in soy sauce and green chillies.

I tried to burn the depression out of him with spice like a zealous preacher.

I was so sure that if he came to the gym he'd feel better. I was adamant that eating bags of sugary crap was contributing to his insomnia. I didn't go on about it daily, but my frequent suggestions were useless, and based on a) a lack of understanding about the illness and b) Rob's inability to talk about how the depression was truly making him feel.

And when the response is: 'I just need to be left alone for a bit' or, worse, no response at all, it takes the thickest of skins not to take that personally. If you love someone, and you are connected by an invisible cord, you feel shut out and rejected.

Worse, you feel helpless because this illness is trying to rot them to death; it is whispering in their ear that they are worthless, that nothing will ever be good again, and you cannot go in there and kick the shit out of it without hurting them in the process.

You also believe that if anyone could coax them out of a depression it should be you. Haven't we been taught, from the moment we are plonked down in front of our first Disney film, that love conquers all?

But when has the love of a person ever been able to do battle with illness?

What we don't realise is this: it's not that they don't *want* to do the things we are asking them to do, it's that they *can't*.

Rob's parents Prue and David live in Orewa, about a thirty-minute drive north from the centre of Auckland. Like other suburbs in the city, the houses are new builds, set neatly on their own plot of land with carefully tended gardens.

The air is clean, the sky wide and blue, shot through with lenticular clouds that form like white, wispy cigars rolling endlessly against the dome.

Orewa started off as a retirement community and, while it is filled with spry elderly folk, property prices in the city are going nuts due to foreign investors buying up houses, so younger commuters are being drawn to the area by osmosis.

The sea, always present in Auckland like a heartbeat, casting the sound of thudding waves and a salt-tipped breeze through nearby homes, is a five-minute walk from their house.

The vast, beautiful beach, which turns golden on a summer's day, is very dear to me. During our first trip to New Zealand in 2013, Rob had flown a week earlier to settle in, as jet lag seemed to affect him more than it did me. He and his father met me in the early morning at the airport, the sky still pink and newborn, the air warm and humid.

As we walked to the car, I saw that the licence plate said 'M1lady'. I looked at Rob.

'It used to belong to Gran,' he said, referring to Prue's mother

*Lena Lynch. Lena was basically the template for all of the Lynch women – strong, fearless and with a sense of humour that could cut you down and make you laugh, so I've been told.*

*Her husband Cletus went through a phase where he thought personalised licence plates would be the next big thing and ordered a bunch of them. When they didn't sell for thousands of dollars – who would've guessed M1lady wasn't a big hit? – they were distributed among the family.*

*'Big Rig' sits on Felicity's jeep while Gabrielle's car is 'Farlap'. There is nothing more satisfying than when you're driving around Auckland and you see Big Rig, M1lady or Farlap parked up and realise someone you know and love is in the area.*

*Rob and I wanted some alone time, so we went for a walk along the beach, holding hands, nattering about what he'd been up to. The sky was like blue glass and the tide had long since tugged the sea back to its furthest point. Tiny white birds darted from one patch of sand to another as if they had a nervous tic.*

*'What are they?' I asked Rob, half-wanting to know, the other half of me just loving that the answer would roll off his tongue so effortlessly.*

*'Oystercatchers,' he replied. 'They look crazed, don't they?'*

*Standing in the living room, where his coffin once sat so we could say goodbye to him, look at the hair on his beard, take in every last detail of his face, remembering the shape of his chest, the curve of his thumb, wishing wishing wishing he'd wake up, please wake up, why won't he wake up, it is impossible to believe that this was barely a year before.*

*With soft carpet under my feet, sunshine flooding into the room and the distant strains of David playing classical music, it doesn't feel like anything bad can happen here.*

*'Tea?' I hear Prue call. 'Yes, please,' I reply.*

*I look at the back garden, at the soaring pohutukawa tree that will burst into flames of red at Christmas time, and if I close my eyes I can almost pretend Rob is just out there on the wooden deck, smoking a cigarette and sitting in the sun.*

*Prue hands me my tea with a smile, and I look at this woman who is full of so much strength and grace she doesn't even realise it. We are about to embark on our first trip without Rob, to Rotorua further south, and, although he isn't here and I miss holding his hand, there is nothing sad about this.*

*That I am here, that his mother is one of my dearest friends, and that I feel as if this is my home, is more than I could have asked for. Despite the terrible events of the last year, we have held on to our love for Rob, and turned it into love for each other, and at times that outshines all of our darkest moments.*

# Chapter Five

Seven nights and eight days had passed since we returned from Sicily in 2012. We had settled back into our lives, dog walking, making dinner, taking out the rubbish, going to work, intermittent insomnia.

I went to the gym and found I couldn't quite catch my breath while on the cross-trainer. This happened sometimes when I was coming down with a virus, so I stopped, went home and didn't think much of it.

Then it happened the next day, and the day after that.

'It's weird,' I said to my dad when we went round there for dinner. 'I don't feel ill, but I just can't seem to take enough air in while I'm on the cross-trainer.'

My dad is a former surgeon-turned-GP, and he asked me to go see my doctor.

So I did, and she said: 'Don't worry, it's probably just a virus.'

'SEE,' I told my dad on the phone.

'Hmm,' he said.

An hour later he called me back. 'Look, you're not going to like this. But tomorrow morning, you're going to go to A&E, and your mother and I will meet you there.'

'But the doctor said it was fine,' I said, growing increasingly angry that I was being ordered about like a child. I didn't have time to go to the hospital; I needed to go to work.

'I'm sorry,' he replied, not sounding remotely sorry at all, 'but I don't know your doctor. We're going to A&E.'

'I can't BELIEVE HIM,' I huffed to Rob.

'Don't worry, honey,' he said, 'I'm sure it's fine.' Rob had a good way of being the calm mirror to my explosive rants.

The next morning, I stomped to A&E and, as I was waiting to be seen, my parents arrived. My dad clicked into doctor mode and went over to talk to the receptionist, his gait strong and purposeful. My mother was what I always needed: comforting, warm, the smell of her, all that comes with nine months of carrying me, baby blankets and milk, happiness, worry and love.

'This is all a waste of time,' I said, my jaw set in a defiant clench.

I was called to a cubicle and explained my symptoms to the doctor. 'Any family history?'

'Not much. History of heart disease and diabetes. Oh, and my mother had a hole in her heart when she was a child.'

The doctor looked at the nurse.

'We're just going to run an ECG on you. Just to check.'

'I've always been fit and healthy,' I said as they made notes on a clipboard.

I sat in the cubicle and was asked some more questions while my parents waited next to me. Had I ever smoked? *Ohgodohgodohgod.*

Yes, of course I had smoked. I bloody loved smoking from the age of fourteen to about twenty-seven.

Davidoffs when I was feeling fancy, Silk Cuts when I was trying to cut down, Benson and Hedges Silver when I was drunk and sloppy, Camels when I was desperate and cadging. But I had quit for the last five years and had done so smug in the knowledge that my parents never had to know. In a time-honoured tradition dating back to my uncles and aunts, Indian children never, ever tell their parents the truth when it comes to smoking.

This was probably not the best time to start telling porkies, though.

'Yes, I used to smoke.'

My parents' eyes goggled. At least it distracted them from going mad with worry.

'Hypocrites,' I said. 'You both smoked.' I looked pointedly at my mother. 'Yes, you too, broncho-lungs!'

The ECG looked into my heart and wrote its findings in sharp, secret zigzags on a page. 'We're now going to run an echo cardiogram,' the doctors announced.

I lay on the table in a dark room, goop spread over my

chest. Then I heard my heart. It spoke to me in desperate thumps, but I couldn't understand what it was saying.

An hour later, I was back in a different cubicle. I felt like this cubicle had moved up a notch in terms of seriousness.

'We need to talk,' said the doctor. She pulled the curtains closed for privacy. Unless she was about to communicate via sign language, I didn't see the point. I could hear the woman next to me being bollocked by her family because she had a drinking problem.

'You have a hole in your heart.'

THUMP.

'It's an inch across and you've had it since birth.'

THUMP.

We all looked at each other, and then at the doctor.

'I don't understand. How am I only finding this out now? I'm thirty-one. When Mum had hers, she couldn't even walk up the stairs when she was a child.'

The doctor explained that a hole in the heart is always congenital, and I'd had it from birth. But presumably the rest of me had been strong enough to keep going, and I'd carried on without even realising the effects of it. But now it had reached the point where the heart couldn't cope any more. It was enlarged, and that hole needed to be closed.

THUMP.

An inch across.

She left the cubicle and my parents' arms swept around me like a ball, and we all cried.

We cried because I had been such a healthy baby, it seemed unlikely I had inherited Mum's hole in the heart so they didn't arrange for me to have a scan.

We cried because if we hadn't caught it when we did, I could have had a stroke.

We cried because until I had an endoscopy, we wouldn't know if I needed open-heart surgery or keyhole. When the doctor explained this, I saw my mother, through her tears, briefly touch the deep scars that ran down the middle of her chest, the marks of a time when life was hammered back into her.

They wanted to keep me in overnight for observation.

My sister came, then my close friends. 'Where's Rob?' they asked. I wondered that too. It had been three hours since Mum called him and told him the news.

When he eventually arrived, he gave me a kiss and stayed while people drifted off back to their homes. I was so pleased to see him. He was the person I found comfort in, who would look after me, nuzzle me and tell me it would be all right.

I was transferred to the cardiac ward, where I was the youngest one there. I caught sight of my reflection. A frightened brown girl cast dark against the white walls, white bed. The sound of ventilators and coughing briefly breaking the silence of people willing their bodies to heal.

'Do you want dinner?' he said when we'd barely settled.

'That'd be nice, thanks,' I replied, part of me wishing we'd had some time to talk before he rushed off. I didn't know if I was being dramatic but it was as if he couldn't bear to be in the same room as me.

He fetched me some noodles, and I'd just finished eating when he said: 'Well, I'd better be off, love. I'll come and fetch you in the morning, all right?'

I didn't want him to go. I didn't understand why he'd taken so long to arrive, and then was so quick to leave. Wasn't he supposed to stay and comfort me? Wasn't that what married people did for each other?

When I returned home the next day, I felt broken. I was quite literally broken – an inch across, in fact. Over the next few months while I waited for the surgery, I couldn't do more than walk. For the first time in my life, my body felt like it was running on a low battery, getting slower and slower. I closed my eyes and thought of all that blood leaking through the wrong side.

Running to the bus stop was out of the question, and I had to figure out other ways to keep fit, so I walked everywhere, went for swims regularly.

My life with Rob during that time was a blur.

Our families were concerned about how he was handling it, but he seemed pretty nonchalant. 'People keep asking me if I'm okay,' he said, 'but I don't see what good worrying will do. I know you'll be fine.'

While I don't remember much, from my diary entries I think that, like the ECG, there were zigzags between the good days and bad. We would have a few that were awful, punctuated by his lack of sleep and communication, and then a few days that by contrast were wonderful, full of affection and love.

There is an entry that says: 'We have become closer than ever. I didn't think it was possible to love him any more than I do, but he is amazing.'

Although the strongest memories are of what Rob didn't do around that time, there are flashes of good ones that I know to be true because that's who Rob was, for most of our relationship. He may have been crap at times with the supermarket shop, or getting out of bed, but he rubbed my back when it was sore.

When we lay in bed and my feet were like ice blocks, he'd let me press them against his legs uncomplainingly so they'd get warm.

When we were snuggled in bed, I'd ask him to get me peppermint tea and a hot water bottle, and he'd do it willingly. When I ordered something from IKEA and got fed up with it, I'd hand him the instructions, a tangle of furniture that was meant to resemble a bookcase and a screwdriver, and he'd get on with it.

In fact, a lot of the house stuff – whether that was moving big boxes around, shovelling shit (he did this, literally, when someone crapped next to our tent at Bestival), walking the dog, carrying the bags and taking out the bins – he took care of. If one of us needed to take the car to the garage or go on a mission that was awkward and needed two bus journeys to get there, he'd do it without so much as a gripe.

But a few days after that diary entry, I wrote the following, and clearly we must have had a conversation in which he talked about being suicidal:

I'm just going to come out and say it: Rob's depression is getting me down. I'm trying, I really am, but the effect of dealing with his stuff and my surgery has just worn me down.

I can't talk to anyone about it either, and that's the hard part. I just didn't think the first year of marriage would be like this. I want him to sleep well and enjoy life but the more time goes on, I wonder if that day is going to come.

I hate the person I become when he's depressed. Needy. Fearful. Unloved. And yet I do know the whole time that it's the disease, he's not being like that on purpose. But it is hard to explain to other people why he's said two words all evening. Or why he sleeps all day. Or why we can't do things because he can't sleep at night.

The endless insomnia, backaches, toothaches, stomach cramps. My God. I know that depression is tunnel vision but I barely register as wallpaper.

And what the fuck do you do when your spouse says they have entertained thoughts of suicide? How the fuck am I supposed to handle that? Something has to change.

I love him so much but I am so tired of feeling resentful and out of my depth.


I don't remember that particular conversation about suicide, but I do know that it was around the time Rob started to talk about the amount of debt he was in. We were talking thousands.

'I don't understand – how did you accrue so much debt?' I asked. He wouldn't let me see his accounts.

'Wedding stuff,' he replied.

'But my parents paid for most of the wedding,' I said, shocked.

He said things mounted up, and he was now crippled by the amount of interest he was paying off on credit cards.

We were in the middle of selling Oakdale Road to buy a new house, but eventually he asked if we could use the equity to pay off his debts (and some of mine from previous years), and we'd rent until we managed to save up enough for another deposit.

In the middle of one of the most difficult times of my life, I realised we had lost our home. I didn't feel I could shout at Rob about it, because I hadn't contributed anything to buying the house. In fact, my irresponsible borrowing around the time of the wedding meant I couldn't help us out either.

By the time my surgery was scheduled – and it was key-hole – I lost sight of what was going on with Rob. I was drawn into fixing my own body, and the huge emotions that came out of that.

I needed my mother more than I wanted Rob. She knew what this felt like, and she provided a comfort no one else could, yet I could see the guilt on her face. She felt it was her fault because I'd inherited the gene. But she wasn't responsible for it any more than Rob's parents were responsible for him having depression.

My mother wasn't expected to live beyond her teenage years. A sickly child, she was one of the first to have pioneering surgery that fixed a hole in the heart. The success rates weren't high, but my mother looked it in the eye and fought through.

Although my procedure was keyhole, and I only spent the night in hospital, it took my body three weeks to recover. It took my mind a lot longer.

During that time spent convalescing at home, I learned a lot about Rob. Despite me being the patient, he spent more time in bed than I did. But when I asked him about it – 'Look, I don't want to piss you off but when are you working? You seem to spend most of your time lying down?' – he got really defensive.

The resentment drifted through the house like dust. Always there, but never so tangible it took form as an argument. For once, I was the one who needed help and looking after, and I didn't feel I could rely on Rob at all.

This is one of the hardest things when it comes to looking

after someone with mental illness. It doesn't matter what problems you have or if you're having a bad day. You have to constantly shelve your emotions because the other person will always need looking after.

When you have the flu, be prepared to put on your coat and drag your diseased, bedraggled ass to the shops to get some Lemsip, because you can't rely on it coming from your other 50 per cent. You're both Florence Nightingale and Universal Soldier, in that you're patient, loving and resilient as hell.

Because when I sat there in bed with no energy, wanting to be alone, not understanding why the fuck my husband was still in bed at 11am when he should have been working, it took every ounce of willpower not to scream: 'IT'S NOT FAIR!'

Then, just when I thought I couldn't take it any more, it just wasn't on, he'd bound into the room with a beautiful, wide smile on his face and talk about the big commission he'd landed, or ask me to go look at baby owls with him in the park.

I mean, seriously, how mad can you be at someone who wants to go see baby owls? But this constant yo-yoing, veering from low to high, meant I wasn't asking the right questions. Before I had long enough to dwell on it, to truly observe what was happening, Rob's tempo would change and it would be all right again.

At the mention of suicide, I know I asked him to go and

see his GP. 'He needs to refer you to a therapist, or to a psychiatrist, Rob.'

When Rob was eventually referred to a psychiatrist, I asked him how it went.

'All right, but I don't think she knows what to do with me.'

'What does that mean?'

'She looked freaked out. I don't think she can handle me.'

I had no idea what this meant.

Then Rob announced the doctor had discharged him. None of this made sense, but he said he was feeling much better.

While I thought I was the one going mad from the constant seesawing between high and low, I wasn't the only person who experienced it. One of his best friends, Jesse, knew exactly what I was going through.

When I first met Rob, he told me about the idea of the Big Family. He said Jesse and he were staunch believers in it. It meant that wherever in the world you were, they would try to put you in touch with someone in that country who would help you out. Whether it was a couch for the night or a shared meal. Then you paid it forward and, inch by inch, the world became a more known place and life became more connected.

When my sister was in New York and in the painful, raw throes of her marriage ending, Rob called upon the Big Family and Jesse immediately put her up in the flat where he was living at the time. It's something that my parents have never forgotten – Jesse is pretty much like a black Vishnu in their eyes. It was little wonder that Jesse would go on to become one of the great loves of myself, and my New Zealand and Indian families.

Rob was introduced to him through a mutual friend named Toby while visiting New York in winter, and he knew Jesse had just been diagnosed with HIV at the age of nineteen. Jesse was angry, and felt like his life held nothing for him any more. 'What was the fucking point?' he said.

But then along came Rob, who pushed himself into his life.

'I was desperately lonely and afraid when I first met Rob,' he told me. 'That's just the truth of the matter. It felt like doors were closing left and right, and what I thought my life was going to be was no longer what it was actually going to be. And that just filled me with emptiness and fear. I think that's important to say, because my relationship with Rob represented options.

'I mean, I know he knew that he pulled me out of a terrifying time in my life, but I don't know if he knew the potential being friends with him showed me. He opened the world to me. By, like, literally taking me around the world and showing me things. But also by harassing me – I mean, I admired him so much, but when I was nineteen I didn't think I was any good, anyone worth being around.

'But Rob would harass me. He'd call me on the phone. He'd email me so often – and I mean, really often, probably like five times a day for fourteen years? Or more. He was the engine of our friendship. And him wanting to be friends with me kind of showed me that I was someone worth being friends with.'

However, he also knew Rob had his moods, and there was something comforting for me in knowing that he absorbed them too. That it wasn't something I'd done or said.

'God, did I know those moods well,' he said. 'He would be excited to see me, then, at the drop of a hat, he would go cold, disinterested, flippant, unkind. But Rob was always like this. And I got used to it – I learned to not take it personally.

'When he shifted, I would shift with him – read with him in silence, try not to annoy him.'

Jesse also dated Mikey, who co-owned the house with Rob. He shared a story about their break-up. For all of Rob's difficulties, and the stress of switching track to keep up with him, it made me cry that someone who was capable of giving both of us such warmth and love was no longer here.

'I remember I had an awful visit to England after Mikey broke up with me,' Jesse said. 'I tried so hard to come back to London and just do the city like I used to, but it wasn't the same and I wasn't the same and I fucking hated it.

'I was sleeping on the couch in the living room and Rob came down early in the morning and kicked me awake and put my head on his lap and sung to me in the early morning light. And it was ... one of the greatest comforts another person has ever given me.'

When I was diagnosed with my hole in the heart and recovering from the surgery, there was a lot that Rob should have done, and didn't. It wasn't about the physical things; it was about being there for me emotionally, and he was absent.

I searched his eyes endlessly to find him. I tried to call him back from the distant place he had gone to, but he was a man travelling his own desert; unreachable, and in a landscape with no map.

I stood at the shoreline alone for most of the time, pinned there by a body that could no longer keep pace, as others swam further out to sea.

But, like he did Jesse, he gave me the greatest moment of comfort I had ever experienced.

On the day of my operation, we woke up early. I remember brushing my hair slowly in front of the mirror, and looking myself in the eye. We got in our Honda that smelled of dog, waved goodbye to Daisy and drove to St Thomas' hospital in Waterloo, where we met my parents.

There was a jolt of excitement and fear. I knew things would never be the same, but I also knew that if my heart had managed to power on with a one-inch gash in it for thirty-one years, then it was remarkable.

But as we sat down in the hospital coffee shop, the smell of beans roasting in the air, the worries of others held in pouches under their eyes, I started to become afraid. I felt small, like I was shrinking to fit in the door to Wonderland.

I breathed the smell of my own mortality and saw the smallness of my own life. Whatever charmed existence I had led was now in the hands of my doctor, his robotics system and a balloon that would swim through my body and clamp a hole in one of my most vital organs.

Rob saw my fear. He looked at me and gestured for me to come over and sit on his chair. I hesitated – my parents were there (we didn't do public displays of affection in front of them) and people would think it was weird; us sitting one in front of the other like we were on a tandem bicycle.

'Just come over,' he said gruffly.

I sat tentatively in front of him. The chair was big enough.

He pulled me in closer and put his arms around me, wrapped me tightly in a circle and kissed the back of my neck. In that moment, it felt like being at the centre of everything. We closed our eyes and went to that place where our love for each other came from.

It was exactly what I needed. I felt safe, I felt loved and I thought, *If this is all there ever is, and that blasted balloon explodes my heart into pieces, this is enough.*

Then I caught Dad's eye.

I was never sure what my dad thought of Rob – he's not a massive fan of tattoos, he was concerned about Rob's depression before we got married, and Rob tended to clonk around their house breaking things and leaving mud everywhere.

But while we don't talk a huge amount, we do often know how the other is feeling without needing to speak.

I sensed Dad nod imperceptibly.

Acknowledgement that whatever his turmoil about the impact Rob's depression was having on me, my father knew that my husband, in that moment, had been what he believed a man should be: protective, attentive and strong.

*Maori legends best paint an understanding of the close relationship between people, earth, sky and water. Rob loved stories about the taniwha, colossal beings of the sea, gods and monsters made of strength, sinew and spine, sometimes benign when acting as protective guardians, sometimes destructive when tossing people down their gullets like oysters.*

*When he was in New Zealand shortly before he died, he mentioned taniwha in one of his emails. I liked to hear about the details of his day.*

Aotea (aka Great Barrier, I am trying to get used to the Maori names for stuff we never used the Maori names for when we were kids) was visible on the horizon as the sun came up, but there was rain coming up from the south, so Hauturu (Little Barrier) was hidden away. I have an image at the moment of Hauturu as a ginormous taniwha in the shape of an octopus, slowly (and balefully, it would have to be balefully) opening its eyes, with the bush proving to be no more than the moss on its (baleful) brow. I imagined it moving slowly towards the harbour, stopping to wrap a ginormous tentacle around the crater of Rangitoto, pulling it into the sea, causing a tidal wave that would push the container ships up against the cliffs, the yachts in the marina up onto the motorway, send seawater frothing. I pictured people standing on Maungauika watching the taniwha follow the wave in and tear down the bridge, before generally eating people and making a menace of itself. Okay, it looked cooler in my head than it does written down.

*Mythology says taniwha can live in the sea or dark caves, but they can also live in rivers. And some say that if a person had dealings with one when they were alive, they may transform into a taniwha when they pass away. I love the idea of a person's soul pouring into a creature of seawater, moving amid the depths of the ocean, gliding over underwater forests of coral.*

*A hundred taniwha are meant to live in the Waikato, which is New Zealand's longest river, each one representing a great Maori chief. As rivers go, it is a powerful spiritual link between the land of the living and the land of the dead.*

*Waikato begins its journey at Mount Ruapehu in the south, winds its way to Lake Taupo (the largest in New Zealand), and then empties into the Tasman Sea. Along its entire 425 kilometres, the speed and landscape can change from sedate water to thundering blue foam crashing over rocks.*

*Prue, David and I are at a café next to a calm part of the river, sipping the best cappuccino in the world. When driving south from Auckland, it's a convenient stop. The reason why it's the best isn't because they use Allpress or beans harvested under the light of a full moon. It's because when I close my eyes and feel a little burst of sweetness as the chocolate dust hits my tongue, I imagine Rob next to me, as he was almost exactly three years ago.*

*It's not sadness, rather an imprint of a time and place before I knew the full truth about what was happening with him.*

*We were all on our way south to Waitomo to look at glow-worms, and he made fun of Prue in the gift shop. 'You're never going to buy anything, Mum,' he hollered as she pottered around the merino slipper section, while David looked patiently on, having done this dance many times before.*

*Now, we are on our way south this time to Rotorua, to the land of sulphur and hot springs. We will always be three, never again four.*

*Although I feel Rob's absence, I wonder if he is a beautiful taniwha, taking a break from swimming with kingfish and thinking about who to eat, and is watching us from the rushes of grass below our window.*

*If Rob is a taniwha, I wonder if he thinks about the only time we visited New Zealand together.*

# Chapter Six

It was 2013 and Rob decided it was time to visit New Zealand for our first trip there as a married couple. As it was my first time, we tried not to pack too much in. So apart from the trip to Waitomo to see the glowworms, we spent the rest of our time in Auckland with the friends he grew up with and his family. Simple walks on the beach, a trip on Wesley's yacht, and nights at Felicity's drinking red wine and eating Otago cheese on her deck.

His younger brothers John and Alan came over for Easter, and we spent some time with them. John looked so much like Rob and his mother, except with a mop of blond hair, and Alan looked very much like David, except with a shaved head and a tree tattoo across his chest.

Rob drank beer every day. I saw the worry work its way onto his parents' faces with each can that was opened, and I sensed a bad history there around his drinking. But what I noticed in New Zealand was that Rob was almost completely different to how he was in England. Grandiose, loud, and with an even bigger swagger. Verging on obnoxious.

I had no problem with my husband having a voice (it was better than his usual long silences) but there was something about it that suggested armour and artifice, a stranger's face stapled onto his real one. A desperate urgency to show how well he was doing, how confident he was.

After one particularly loud monologue (which involved him talking over people), I looked at him and said: 'Seriously, dude, who are you?'

He talked endlessly about his insomnia and borrowed sleeping pills; I remember Prue approaching me to ask if he was all right. I think she was worried he was verging on mania.

'He's fine,' I reassured her. In hindsight, I realised I was basing my diagnosis purely on Rob's assertion that he was fine.

One sunny afternoon, we were driving into Auckland city from Orewa, in his uncle Chris's clapped-out Honda, with the windows rolled down, listening to nineties rock on Radio Hauraki. Rob was going to show me a potted history of Robert Owen Bell circa 1987–95, from old houses to favourite teenage haunts.

Green Day's *Dookie* had just come on.

'So, I just found out L is addicted to heroin,' he said casually.

'What?!' I yelled and turned down the radio. L was some-one very close to us.

'Did you talk to him? Tell him under no uncertain terms to quit?'

'No, how could I? I'd be a hypocrite.'

'Yeah, but you're not a junkie. You don't use heroin. Surely that's worth saying?'

He shrugged and looked straight ahead. 'I don't think anything I say will make a difference,' he replied.


Six months after this conversation was Rob Broke My Heart Day.

It started as a fairly normal day. Well, normal for us; he had stayed in bed the whole of Saturday. We had moved to a big flat in Streatham after selling Oakdale, and I spent all day on my own, doing the food shop, cleaning the house, in between trying to cajole him to get up.

I remember sitting on the sofa – which my parents had bought us for our wedding – and thinking, *This is the third weekend in a row where he has just lain in bed.*

By Sunday, I was furious. He was still in bed. The sheets stank of sweat, sheets I would have to change because I couldn't sleep in a dirty bed.

I couldn't even bring myself to talk to him. I was so mad. *He always does this. What is actually wrong with him? Why is he so goddamn lazy? Doesn't he care about me at all?*

So I left the house to go to the gym. It was a bright, cold day in October – the cusp of autumn and winter. I had an amazing workout, and I vowed that if he hadn't got up by the time I returned, I was going to kick off.

Of course, he hadn't got up by the time I returned.

He said hello to me from the bedroom. I ignored him. 'Baby,' he said.

He kept saying it. 'Baby. Please talk to me. Please.' All the while still lying down in bed.

I went into the bedroom, now so angry I was ready to pack a bag and leave.

I sat down on the edge of the bed and looked into his pale, sweaty face. 'I'm sick of this. I'm fucking sick of this,' I said. 'You have to tell me what's wrong. I can't help you if I don't know what's going on with you.'

He gazed at me. His face washed clean of any energy, his eyes scared. His mouth silent.

I felt disgusted and fed up. 'You know what, Rob? Forget it.'

I made as if to get up and he said: 'I'm worrying about money.'

It wasn't good enough.

'I don't get it. You're working all the time – where is your money going? You don't spend it on yourself. You're wearing clothes that are literally falling apart. You don't go anywhere. What is going on?'

I don't know why he chose that moment. We must have had this conversation so many times, about money and him being in bed, his insomnia and so on, that it felt like a tape stuck on a loop.

Maybe there was just something different about that day.

Maybe he was simply tired of pretending his life was okay when he was actually smoking his future away in his dank little bathroom at the other end of the flat.

But that day, he actually told me the truth.

'I'm a heroin addict.'

I didn't know – outside of having a fever – that it was possible for someone's words to make you feel cold and hot at the same time. That you could feel as if your future had contracted to a pinpoint but at the same time had grown unbearably long in the face of the battle ahead.

I didn't even utter the words 'Are you joking?', like people do in the movies. Because I knew it wasn't a joke. In the first few seconds of knowing, it immediately answered a lot of the questions around his behaviour, his physical state of being, his inability to do even the simplest of tasks, his total and utter retreat from life.

'I feel sick,' I said and ran downstairs to my home office. I remember facing the wall and dry heaving. I remember going back upstairs and asking him questions like a robot.

'How long?'

'Three years.'

'Why have I never seen needle marks on your arms?'

'Not all heroin users inject, I smoked it on foil so you wouldn't know.'

'WAS THAT WHY THERE WAS NEVER ANY FUCKING FOIL IN THE HOUSE?'

'Yes.'

'Were you an addict before we got married?'

A pause. 'Yes.'

'So this whole time you've been lying to me and pretending it was depression, when you were actually a junkie?'

A pained look in his eyes at the use of that word.

'Not exactly. My depression *has* been really bad.'

'How bad?'

'I tried to kill myself six months ago when I went camping.'

Oh my God. Oh my God. What the fuck was happening? How had my life gone from *The Good Life* to *The Wire* in the space of five minutes?

'How?'

'I tried to gas myself with the car's exhaust in a tent but Daisy pulled me out.'

'Were you going to leave a note?'

He held his hands out. 'What could I say that would make it okay? At least that way you wouldn't know I was a drug addict.'

I felt like I was going to explode. Everything was so intense; the fury about being lied to met with the cold, horrifying realisation that Rob had been so close to dying. That I would have received a knock on the door from the police saying he was dead, and I would have had no idea why.

The next few moments were a blur. I think I said all the

things an addict's wife or husband would say. I'd like to think this isn't stereotyping because the behaviours around addiction are often so similar: lying, manipulation, chaos, pain, sadness, disbelief.

I asked him how he could do that to me. How could he lie to me if he loved me? How could he put me through this? How could he leave me on my own for so long? How could he dupe me like that before we got married? How could he make me feel I was the one going mad with paranoia?

'WHAT KIND OF MONSTER DOES THAT TO SOMEONE THEY LOVE?' I shouted.

I don't know in what order he said the following, but he told me it wasn't that straightforward, that I was the single most important thing to him and that he'd tried to quit in secret. He went through withdrawal hundreds of times; he just couldn't stick to it.

He said he lived with this pressure, the stress of feeling sick that he was lying to me every single day. He had sold the house to pay off his drug debts, and then had just racked them up again. So, in addition to being a drug addict, he was also back in debt to the tune of £30,000.

When I asked why he hadn't told me before it got so bad, he answered simply: 'I knew how you felt about drugs. You would have left me.'

So he'd attempted to quit without me knowing or ever finding out that he was this person. But of course, as any healthcare professional will tell you, you cannot do recovery alone.

But to him, the person he had become – lying to everyone, losing all his money and his house – went against the grain of everything he believed in. He was meant to look after me and cherish me and, in his eyes, he was failing in that every day.

He wrote me a letter, about the lying and drug use:

Why did I lie? Part in fear at your reaction, in fear of disappointing you. Because one of the nastier things about this addiction is it makes lying the default position, and the lie on the tip of your tongue slips out, the lie is told and every moment that passes, you're building a pyramid of lies and the truth slips further away.

And also that original grand error. The never-valid self-delusion that I can somehow fix everything myself and it will all disappear as if it never happened.

In the days that followed Rob's confession, I was haunted by memories of events altered in the light of what I now knew.

The sound of crinkling foil that Rob said was a newspaper as he shooed me away from the bathroom door. Endless trips to the corner shop for Lucozade when he was actually buying drugs. Inexplicable disappearances late at night without telling me, later explained as going to the petrol station for cigarettes.

But one of the most unforgivable: the real reason why he

was so late coming to the hospital on the day I was diagnosed with my heart problem.

I think he expected me to leave him. But there was absolutely no question of it even though he had let me down so badly.

He needed understanding and love and I was going to help him. When I calmed down, I realised how awful it must have been for him. I'm not saying he deserved full absolution, but he lived with that feeling of shame, guilt and self-loathing every night, for so long. I couldn't stand that he'd been in that much pain.

I didn't want him to carry it any longer.

There was no way I was going to let the person I loved most in the entire world die in a fucking tent, alone, because he was too scared to ask for help.

I just wished he had told me sooner.

Although my world was blown apart, I couldn't tell my friends. I certainly couldn't tell my parents who – while no strangers to addiction in our family – didn't understand why addicts couldn't just 'stop'. How could these two people, who attended our wedding on that beautiful, bright summer's day and watched as he promised to protect me, ever forgive him?

I put off calling them in the first few days after Rob's confession. Their voices reminded me of a time and an innocence I no longer had. I felt like I didn't deserve their love.

Walking down Streatham high street I saw couples walking side by side, and I was filled with such jealousy, such longing to be like them. I felt as if I was holding something so heavy, I didn't know how I could bear it.

I had to meet up with friends and smile. Chatter on about work, when inside I was dying. 'We're thinking of buying a house next year,' I would hear myself saying, when we could barely make rent.

No one knew that the equity of our house had gone to pay huge debts, money I now knew had passed through Rob's bloodstream, into his brain and sweated into our sheets. Every time I washed those sheets, the money we earned disappeared in a froth of water and suds.

Rob had spent the last three years leading a double life and now I found myself doing the same. When everyone asked how I was, I said I was fine. So that became my refrain. How are you? 'I'm fine.' How's Rob? 'Oh, he's fine. We're both fine.'

Behind closed doors I struggled with forgiveness and the constant fear that he would die if I strayed too far from him. Never has the word 'fine' been so far removed from its actual meaning.


All my life, I've lived with some sort of duality. I didn't even realise that until recently.

My family consists of Mum, Dad and Priya, who is older than me by four years. When we were little, we lived in

Maidstone and my dad drove a red Golf Volkswagen while working as an orthopaedic surgeon. My mum made the slog up to London every day to work for the Inland Revenue.

We had an apple tree in our garden, and I remember one winter that was so cold it dressed our little kingdom in snow. Hundreds of icicles appeared along the gutters in long spikes, as if someone had pressed pause on a cascade of water.

As a child, my sister was sent to live in India with my mother's parents – they lived in a flat at the bottom of a compound in Mangalore, home to summer rain and red sandstone. I think this was because my mum couldn't look after the two of us with her job, and they needed the money. I remember my sister's absence like a deep ache, but then my parents made the decision to move back to India.

Perhaps I had shown an unhealthy attachment to fishfingers over chicken curry, or maybe it was the English accent coming out of my brown mouth. Or maybe they were dismayed that I was becoming like my school friends, more concerned with toys than good grades. In any case, they decided we needed to be more Indian.

In India, it didn't matter if you had an entire stable of My Little Ponies – bad grades meant you were a bozo, and bozos didn't have friends. So the plan was that my mother and I would move first to our grandparents' house in Mangalore, then my dad would sell the house they owned in Maidstone and move once the sale had completed.

I was seven, and the mosquitoes greeted my arrival with

enthusiasm. It was also a time when I learned that a lot of people take electricity for granted. We sat there in the dark during one of the many power outages, candles lighting a room (at that age, they weren't romantic, just spooky, especially if a careless uncle had allowed you to watch *A Nightmare on Elm Street* ten years too early), insects humming in our ears, the fans silent and impassive in the face of sweat dribbling down our faces.

Once the joy of seeing my sister – I touched her face to check she was real and offloaded all the presents I'd carefully picked in the hope she would love me more if they were the right kind – had faded, it was replaced with the ache of missing my dad.

But in between the lack of Dad, there were other things to consider.

Namely school.

School in Mangalore was a sea of brown bodies everywhere – I had never seen so many other girls who looked just like me. It was strange at first because it seemed so familiar, I felt so at home, and I didn't have to think about anything there. I wasn't split in two. I didn't have to explain to my school friends about Indian food – it was like a hive mind working in unison.

The only thing that didn't fit in was my English accent. The other kids weren't mean about it – they just mentioned it as a matter of fact. 'Your accent is different.'

I didn't want to be different. I had big ole green eyes stuck on a coffee-coloured face – that was different enough for me. I didn't want this accent trapped inside my mouth like an Everlasting Gobstopper.

I dropped it quickly; it came very easily to me. Eventually we moved from Mangalore to the garden city of Bangalore – before it turned into a giant shopping mall and still had greenery and beautiful old colonial houses.

We waited for my dad to arrive. One year passed, and then two.

Recession was blowing through Britain like an unforgiving wind, and he was finding it hard to sell the house. Two years turned into five and, by the end, my mother had had enough. It was time for our family of three to move back to England and become four once again.

Moving to England as an on-the-cusp teenager with scrawny limbs, a predilection for thick, white slouch socks, a lingering affection for teddy bears and a clinginess to one's sister and mother was not a recipe for success. In fact, I'm impressed I didn't have the shit kicked out of me on the first day of school.

But that accent, now with its hard emphasis on the d's, t's and rolling r's had to go again. This time the kids weren't matter of fact; they looked at me as if I had just emerged from under a smelly, curry-stained rock and, as far as they were concerned, I could pack my bags and crawl back under there.

So I quickly wallpapered over a new accent and made friends. A big group of friends, actually. We were all into a mix of punk, goth, metal and indie music, and we'd spend hours on a weekend fighting over who discovered our favourite bands first, mooching around and looking at boys.

I was lucky my parents didn't own a corner shop and expect me to heft boxes of Fanta around. I mean, the Indian shopkeeper did become a stereotype on mainstream television, but that was not to say there weren't loads of them around.

But this is when I truly became aware of this double life I led. I went to great pains to hide my English accent from my parents.

The Telephone – and I refer to it in the reverential capital as it was a crucial conduit to the outside world (in actual fact, my friends' own unexciting family homes) – sat in a weird annexe at the front of the house, separated from the kitchen and lounge by a glass door. When friends called, I'd slam the door shut and talk like the Artful Dodger. I'd get extremely twitchy if my mother walked anywhere in the vicinity of the door lest she caught wind of my accent.

Food was a biggie. I was aware, from visiting other people's houses, how badly Indian food ponged. It sewed itself into curtains, coats and hair and proclaimed loudly on public transport: Hey! I eat curry for breakfast, lunch and dinner!

I would edge away from these people as fast as possible. *I eat chicken nuggets, unlike this curry muncher*, my eyes pleadingly conveyed.

I remember when my cover was blown.

A friend had come over to stay. Let's call her B.

B wanted some chocolate, so I got some from the veg box in the fridge. She ate it, job done. Then two weeks later, another friend, C, said: 'Look, I don't want to make you feel bad, but B was saying something mean about you.'

In hindsight, I don't know why the fuck girls do this to each other. They are in the possession of some hurtful information that will do the listener no good, yet blurt it out like dal in an American's gut.

'Oh yeah?' I said as nonchalantly as I could. Of course, there was nothing casual about this. My brain went into panic mode.

C clearly wanted to offload this information. She opened her mouth and out came the dal.

'Yeah, she said she went round your house and you gave her some . . . chocolate.'

'Okay,' I replied, a bit relieved but irritated at the anticlimax of this story. From C's *sotto voce* you'd have thought B had come across the monkey-head stew from *Indiana Jones and the Temple of Doom*.

'That was it?' I asked.

C wrinkled her face. 'B said it tasted funny.'

'What kind of funny?'

'Just . . . you know, weird.'

After school, I went home and conducted an investigation via an examination of the veg box. Turns out some bright spark had placed the chocolate next to onions, garlic and ginger – the triad of ingredients that make up almost every single Indian dish. And although it didn't make sense, I felt ashamed. Ashamed that my Indianness had permeated Cadbury's finest chocolate produce, and now they knew OH MY GOD WE ATE ONIONS! AND GARLIC!

After Chocolategate, I did everything to expunge this from the memory of my friends. I ate chips-in-a-bag every day (thankfully, my mother was not the kind of person who would pack Indian food for lunch). My cockney accent went up a notch.

I even took it so far that I turned into that most niche of creatures: the brown goth. Credit goes to my parents for not batting an eyelid when I emerged like a grumpy, squashed butterfly from my room, dressed in fishnets, PVC skirt, something resembling lingerie and a floor-length leather jacket. I doubt there were many other Asian mums and dads in the nineties who went with their daughters to buy steel-toecap boots for their birthday presents.

But there were strains. They would not let me hang out in town centres after dark in the same way my friends did. They made it clear in no uncertain terms that if I did stay out after dark, not only would I be grounded but THE NIGHT WAS FRAUGHT WITH DANGERS. In fact, it's amazing I don't have a nervous twitch when the sun goes down, considering I grew up before the era of mobile phones and factoring in the (un)reliability of public transport to get home on time.

If we went to gigs, they insisted on a parent picking us up

(from London, no less). And they wanted me to phone them after the gig, which in those days involved finding a grotty payphone in a sea of sweaty people outside the venue.

They absolutely wouldn't allow boyfriends, at least until I was eighteen.

If I'm giving the impression that I stuck to all/any of the rules, I should probably say (sorry, Mum and Dad) that I really didn't. The person taking us home after gigs was our friend National Rail, and I had my first boyfriend at fourteen. So I led two completely separate lives. Whenever I saw the two worlds colliding (parent-teacher meetings, car pool), I would get very anxious and jittery.

Duality may buy you temporary peace in the present, but it always catches up with you eventually, and it always comes at a price. Although I tried to escape leading a double life, here I was again, like I had never left.

As far as I was concerned, when we stood up there in front of our loved ones on a summer's day in July 2011 and exchanged our vows, I was signing up to a life of beautiful boring coupledom, kids and happiness.

I walked in front of every single person I loved, and told the man I loved more than anyone that I would be there for him in sickness and in health, and that we would still be fighting over comic books when we were eighty. We swore our loyalty and fidelity to each other.

The truth about marriage is that, beyond the fairy tale, making all those promises in front of so many witnesses means it's harder to walk away when things get tough.

That may sound cynical, and though I stayed with Rob and tried to help him because first and foremost I loved him (and when you love someone you cannot sit idly by while they are slowly killing themselves), I also know that declaring our wedding vows in front of friends and family was an important part of what kept us together.

But this also placed a huge amount of pressure on how we portrayed ourselves to our loved ones.

It is no coincidence that, after marriage, friends stop talking to each other about their relationships. We don't want to admit anything is wrong because we have signed up for life. We want to be continuously surprised and enchanted by our partners but we also want stability and reassurance from them. We may not like to admit it, but we look to them to fix what is wrong in our lives and when they can't (because no one can do that for us), we feel disappointed.

And we don't want to be a statistic – one of the Divorced – because, God knows, there are so many of them. So we fudge the truth a little bit when people ask us if we're okay.

When I think about my life with Rob, there is nothing I wouldn't give for one more day before he told me the truth about what was really going on with him. A day when I could still exist in a world where happy endings came true and love saves the day.

I'm not greedy. I don't even want one of the good days, like when he bought me an Ajit Kumar Das painting of six cows for my birthday and we had dinner at Chez Bruce, giggling because we ordered exactly the same thing.

I'll take one of the days when he couldn't get out of bed. Or even the day Daisy had an accident in the woods and lost an eye, and we had to drive her to the animal hospital where I cried in the car park as he lifted her gently out of the boot.

The memories came relentlessly, like sheets of binary code rewriting our marriage, personal moments, everything I knew about him.

I would wake up and, in the first few wonderful seconds, I didn't remember. Then it would sit on my chest like a boulder.

*It's not fair.*

The part I had most trouble with was not being told before we got married. Because although I knew I would have married him regardless of how bad I knew things could get with the depression, he got married with a lie in his heart.

'You would've left me,' he pleaded.

'You didn't give me a chance,' I replied.

For a time, I took down the photo of us on our wedding day, me in a blue dress, him in a grey suit, looking at each other and smiling. It was a reminder that I was fooled. That one of us knew the truth and one of us didn't.

At times, the grief for that girl, the one who didn't know, the one whose biggest worry was about her career or her Friday-night plans, was so overwhelming that it threatened to consume me. I hated her. I hated her naivety; I hated her happiness and ignorance.

Before all of those feelings had a chance to coalesce into rage, I knew that if I left him or if we didn't act quickly, there was a very real chance Rob would take his own life. There was no time for anger or pity. We needed to kick-start his recovery.

'What do you want to do?' I asked him. 'Every clinic I've called thinks we're mad for not putting you on methadone. They said the success rate without it was about 5 per cent.'

'I don't want to go on methadone,' he said, anguished. 'I just don't want to be an addict. I hate it. I hate it.'

Suboxone – available only in the US – was another replacement that he had obtained through means I chose not to ask about, but the side-effects wiped him out. They could include: tongue pain, redness or numbness inside your mouth, constipation, mild nausea, vomiting, headache, sleep problems (insomnia), increased sweating, swelling in your arms or legs.

'Do you think you can do this without methadone?'

'Yes, absolutely. I spoke to Dr _____ and we laid out our plan. I go cold turkey and you take everything – car keys, wallet and my phone. I go to Narcotics Anonymous, I have zopiclone in case I can't sleep, and I've started the round of antidepressants he wants to put me on.'

'Okay. Well, then. Fuck them, honey. We'll be the 5 per cent, okay?'

He laid out the following:

# ROB'S NEW REGIME

- Attend more than five NA meetings a week, turn up early, share at every meeting. Soak up every benefit I can from the programme.
- Get a sponsor within two weeks and fully take advantage of this part of the programme.
- Call someone from NA every day and text at least two people – and keep a record in my diary of who I speak to.
- Get up at 8am every day without fail and no matter how I'm feeling. Have one cup of coffee, shower, shave EVERY DAY and walk the dog before work.
- No more smoking cigarettes.
- Eat three meals a day.
- Go to church twice a week.
- This week organise Yoga, Wing Chun and perhaps Tai Chi? Go to the gym at least once a week with _____, cutting the cycle of not exercising.
- Purchase home urine tests and take in front of Poorna every two days; this will sort out any bother about my wallet. Access to money won't be a problem if I'm able to prove I'm clean on a literally day-to-day basis.
- If I am struggling with my mental health, contact Dr _____ that day.
- Talk to Jesse about how I am feeling. Make an

agreement with Jesse to check in by email every day and let him know where I am at.

- Take the remaining steps necessary to sort out my finances and tell Poorna exactly what is happening.

By the end of week two, only three of these things had happened.

When it comes to drugs knowledge, my life is partitioned into two sections: before I knew, and after I knew. Before, I had no knowledge of serious drug use. I didn't know what to look for, and when I did get suspicious and asked questions, Rob would effortlessly lie about it or make me think I was being paranoid.

Although I was angry at Rob and I knew diddly-squat about heroin, I was aware that he needed support, not judgement. Love, not recrimination. It was only natural that my feelings of anger needed an outlet, so I directed them at myself.

'I'm a fucking IDIOT,' I raged. 'I brought this on myself. How could I not know? What kind of buffoon doesn't know that her husband is a HEROIN ADDICT?'

'Look, addicts lie,' he said with infuriating self-awareness and calm. 'We manipulate. You didn't know because I was really good at keeping it from you.

'I'm so sorry for what I've done to you, and I can only beg for your forgiveness, but you can't blame yourself. I did this. *Me.*'

I always wondered how it was possible that when a person

died of drug use their partner could claim not to know. I'm living proof that it's possible. That your love for someone simply could not take you to the darkest place it needed to go, where a part of them shivered in shame.

The only person who made me feel like I wasn't going mad was Jesse.

'I remember the first time Rob and I talked about heroin,' he said, when I asked him if he knew Rob had a drug problem.

'He and I were joking about something, sitting on his couch, and he said something along the lines of "maybe a little bit of the old brown" and (this is how stupid I am) I thought he was making some sort of racist joke and I asked him what he was talking about.

'And he responded with something like, "Jesus, Jesse, I'm talking about smack." And then I was like, "Oh. *Oh.*" And then things got a bit serious and I asked him if he really did that. And he was sort of cavalier and said, "Yeah, casually."

'And I said: "No one does heroin casually. You really need to not do that shit, man. It's terrible. It destroys people's lives." And he must have said something to brush me off, or joke about it.

'That was probably the first and last time we spoke about it. Until he called me years later and told me he had a problem, I assumed he had it all under control. Because that fit my perception of him. And probably also because it was the easiest thing to believe.

'But the real question is – what did you really know? And I feel like the answer to that is: everyone knew everything. And no one knew anything.

'I mean, I might have been one of Robby's more innocent friends that he hid shit like this from, but I feel like somewhere deep inside, I knew something wasn't right.'

After he died, some people told me they knew about Rob's addiction all along, not because he told them, but because they weren't innocent lambs like Jesse and me and saw things we didn't. They didn't say anything at the time, and as a result felt guilt I said was not theirs to carry. They didn't put themselves in this position, Rob did.

Now I'm like the Supernanny of drugs.

I know the behaviours; the chaos has a particular pattern, pieces of the jigsaw that just won't fit. And I know what is inevitably going to happen to that person if they don't recognise they have a problem, and they don't seek help.

A lot of my first month with Rob's recovery was spent trying to come to terms with what I *thought* I knew about drug addicts, and what I needed to find out because, hey, turns out what I thought I knew was bullshit.

Despite how prevalent in society drug misuse is, addicts are most often portrayed in polarised situations. You have the shambling addict outside a mainline train station, homeless, his or her eyes gaunt and empty, dirty fingernails.

Then, at the opposite end of the spectrum, you have the celebrity addict. The starlet or A-lister who crashes and burns and ends up in rehab. This person's broken relationship with themselves is front-page news. Then when they die, the world mourns. There are six-page obituaries, memes and columns. Followed by the inquest. Everyone hangs on the results in case the cause of death wasn't drug addiction. Everyone hopes it isn't, because in their eyes that's a different kind of death, a less worthwhile death.

When the shambling addict is found dead, no one cries. No one wonders about the terrible journey they took, to make it from someone's son or daughter to an unloved corpse garlanding the damp corners of urban living. *They brought it on themselves.*

But the celebrity addict acts as a leveller. This was a person who had success, money and family, and because we live in a society that believes money, family and status protect you from bad things, the realisation hits home that *it could happen to your family too.*

How we view drug misuse in society is mostly wrong. A report called 'Taking a New Line on Drugs', written in 2016 by two of the leading health bodies in the UK, sums it up perfectly: 'Drugs are not just substances that are currently illegal. They include socially embedded legal substances, such as alcohol and tobacco, used by the majority of people in the UK. Drugs strategy must reflect this reality, and not create artificial and unhelpful divisions.'

I have plenty of friends and family who don't see tobacco addiction or alcoholism as being as bad as heroin or cocaine use, but the fact is, all drug addiction is the same.

Alcohol and tobacco are more costly to the NHS than all of the class A drugs combined; tobacco kills the most.[3] But somehow, cigarettes and booze are okay because they are socially acceptable. And they are socially acceptable because they are legal, despite being more lethal than the drugs we have been taught to fear since we were kids.

While I knew there were alcoholics in my family, I didn't really know of any drug addicts. Many of us view alcoholism as 'not great' but tend to tolerate it. In fact, I've seen people give well-known alcoholics drinks at parties. Would you hand a coke addict a line of cocaine? Of course not, but the two are the same.

The drug report calls our view of addiction 'simplistic' and that it certainly is.

Before I found out about Rob, I viewed all addicts in the same way: broken and weak. I saw only in black and white. How could it not be weakness? Why couldn't they control themselves? Because when you look at what addicts become – and, really, there are only ever three outcomes: recovery, prison or death – why would anyone choose that for themselves?

One of the things people have most difficulty in understanding about addiction is *why* the person can't just stop – and this was also the reason I couldn't really talk to my friends and family about Rob.

Dr William Shanahan, medical director and consultant psychiatrist at the Nightingale hospital in London, who has had thirty years' experience in dealing with addiction, told me that when it came to opiates, it didn't matter about the environment the person grew up in. It wasn't about a weakness in character. That sometimes, regardless of their family background or the amount of money they earned, they used drugs for a number of reasons, one of them being self-medicating depression and anxiety.

His words reminded me of something Prof. Williams said about the premise of addiction being part medication. 'The rest of us don't see what's going on and don't even want to understand what's in the mind of somebody who feels completely stuck to a pattern of behaviour.'

Opiates in particular are used to numb feeling or to fill an emptiness caused by something else, and considering his history with depression it should have been severely worrying to me that Rob had been struggling with drug use for twenty-five years. More so that it had taken over two decades for him to actually realise he was an addict, and was no longer – if ever he had been – someone doing drugs recreationally.

In society, addiction is more of a taboo than depression, yet the two share similarities: judgement from other people; misinformation around what it is; and they both originate in the brain.

Mix the two of them together, and no wonder there is little to no understanding in society about people who self-medicate a mental illness with drugs or alcohol. Who on earth would feel comfortable talking about their problem with friends over tea?

And perhaps the stigma that drives this need for concealment is the hardest aspect of addiction.

I could handle shutting myself behind a glass door and talking in a whisper so that my parents wouldn't hear my English accent. That was of my choosing.

But when you are the loved one who deals with an addict? None of it, the lies and duality, is your choice, but the burden is almost as heavy and exacting as it is for the addict.

In Rotorua, on my trip with Prue and David, I see things resembling the painting of a dream. At Waimangu, streams of steaming water at the hot springs; algae, orange like a bright sunrise shot through with clouds of emerald greens; a lake of startling blue rimmed in white silica; tiny pipes of fumaroles blowing puffs of steam as if the earth was enjoying an after-dinner cigarette.

Walking around the bush that surrounds the valley, Prue takes a picture of me against a wall of tree ferns, captured in a wave of mist rolling across bubbling lakes. I look as if I could disappear, slip through a tear in the world to another dimension.

We're here because I have never seen volcanic hot springs. The reek of sulphur permeates the town, and, before we left Auckland, everyone said: 'Oh, you get used to it after a while.'

As fascinating as the hot springs are (and no, you don't get used to the smell), the place I love most is the redwood forest, Whakarewarewa. I've always been fascinated by redwoods but have never seen them up close.

These ones are a long way from home, imported from California in the 1900s as part of an early trial, and are among the few trees, along with English oak, Douglas fir and Japanese larch, to survive the planting spree.

The main section of them is in a memorial grove which takes about thirty minutes to walk around, and there is an extra thirty-minute walk if you want to spend more time among the ferns sprinkled at the foot of the trees, their delicate little leaves starkly contrasted against the soaring height and silence of the redwoods. When we enter the grove, the air becomes heavy; everything slows down. The trees demand it. They have spent far more time than us on earth, and they will continue to do so when we are in the ground.

These huge, wooden pillars stretching up to the heavens, their branches streaming against the sky like hair caught in a breeze, push our perspective beyond our current point of pain, beyond our grief that at times feels like this is all there will ever be.

Everything feels primordial here, prehistoric, the scent of earth in my nostrils, and a stillness in my body save for a long, slow thump of the forest's heartbeat, which reminds me of the first time I listened to my heart after it was fixed, the most beautiful sound I had ever heard.

But I also feel something else. As the worlds between old and new shift, the memories that the three of us are creating in the absence of Rob, I feel caught between the rate of time that passes in the world as we know it, and the rate of time as these trees know it.

I don't believe in an afterlife, but I feel Rob so strongly in this place. I feel as if the answer to him is somewhere here, one hand on my heart, and one hand reaching towards the unknowable, wherever he has slipped through to.

It is a feeling so powerful, the grief that I cannot go to where he has gone almost brings me to my knees. I ask Prue and David *if they mind me walking the rest of the track alone, and they nod with concern and kindness.*

*When I can no longer see them, I start crying. Through my tears I see ferns as far as the eye can see. I know from the brochure that these could be silver ferns, palm leaf ferns, black ferns.*

*And nothing will replace Rob, who would have taken pictures of them, been able to tell us exactly which was which, and explain their Latin name, their Maori name, where they normally grow and, in doing so, make our understanding of the world a little bit more beautiful, and a little bit wider.*

# Chapter Seven

For six months every Saturday morning after Rob told me about his addiction, I drove to a tiny building with blue glass windows in Forest Hill.

I'd kiss Rob and wish him a good time at his NA meeting, which started at 11am in Brixton. When he went to NA, he was often the only person in the room who still had a partner and one of the few who still had a job. Anyone who had a partner most likely met them after recovery; their previous relationships had not survived the rollercoaster of addiction.

I'd put on comfortable clothes, and carry something I could twist in my hands or hold close for comfort. Then I'd leave my home at 9.30am after a cup of tea, and I'd think about the two hours that lay ahead.

To stop myself going mad with the double life that had been pressed upon me without my permission, I realised I needed to talk to someone about what was going on.

When you're in a marriage with an addict, at some point you will have to deal with their lying on a regular basis. But it's not just their lies; it turns you into a liar too. It is a bitter pill, and swallow it you must.

Mal thought I was at the gym, my parents that I was busy cleaning the house. Priya knew the truth but had no way to guide me through this situation.

After desperate phone calls to my local council, I found that there was no support for the loved ones who look after addicts. We're the ones who keep them fed, endlessly support them and defend their honour when everyone else doubts they are worth anything at all, yet no help was forthcoming.

When I made an appointment with Lambeth council to talk about this travesty, they invited me to their headquarters in Vauxhall and told me that, due to budget cuts, they had no funding to keep a support group going. 'But you're welcome to start your own,' they suggested.

Great, because I had oodles of time what with working, maintaining my own sanity, lying to my family and friends, and keeping my husband in recovery. Considering how much is spent on drug addiction (including alcohol) in the UK – £15.4 billion – you'd think maybe someone would have the sense to support people like me who actually did still have jobs and were trying to help with recovery. I had to find out the hard way about the cost and reality of supporting a spouse with addiction issues.

POORNA BELL

Many phone calls later, I eventually managed to find a support group in a different borough, run by Donna, a woman whose kindness, empathy and firmness got me through the first six months.

On my first day, I felt like tracing paper. Ashamed and lost, see-through, with no language to describe how I was feeling. The daily conflicts, the yearning for our old life, my sadness for Rob and for myself.

In between going to NA and visiting his doctors, I saw how desperately he clung to redemption, and how tightly I held him so that he wouldn't disappear down a crack. We tried to resurrect our life day by day, dinners spent in front of the TV watching zombie films, walks with Daisy. But we knew something huge had shifted.

Rob thought I didn't notice but I knew how carefully he watched me from the corner of his eyes, wondering and waiting to see if I would leave. In disbelief that he had told me everything and I hadn't left yet.

And I'm sure, at this point in the story, you're thinking: *How on earth could you forgive him? How could you carry on as if nothing happened?*

And my answer is: Has the person you love most in the world ever said they were going to kill themselves, and, aside from the many other reasons contributing to that state of mind, one was because they didn't want you to know who they truly were?

And if you had a chance to give that person redemption,

so that they never felt so desperate as to try to gas themselves to death, are you telling me you wouldn't take it?

Whatever punishment I could dole out, whatever judgements I laid at Rob's feet, they would never, ever come close to what he was putting himself through. And even at that point, without all the knowledge I have now gained about addicts, drug use, suicide and mental health, I was able to understand that much.

There is such a stigma around addiction that addicts and the loved ones in their lives can rarely talk to anyone else about it.

My first support group meeting took place in a sunlit room. We sat on chairs in a circle after making tea and grabbing a croissant to eat in our laps. This was called the 'check-in', where you gave your name and a brief description of why you were there.

Newcomers, as in other support groups, were always given priority. I could see the circle move slowly towards me. Mothers of alcoholics, husbands of crack cocaine addicts, wives of crystal meth users. My face grew hot.

*I don't want to do this. I shouldn't have to be here.*

But if I didn't share, the time would be wasted. And I'd have to wait another seven days before I could talk to someone else about it. So I pulled up my words that lay sunk, like stones at the bottom of a lake.

'My husband told me last week that he was a heroin addict.

He was an addict before we got married, he kept it from me. I don't know how I am going to forgive him, but I want to. I'm so ashamed. I can't tell my family. I love him so much but I don't know how to get through this.'

I couldn't stop crying. It felt like I would never stop crying, that it was coming from a tap jammed open, and it wouldn't cease until I ran dry. Then someone handed me a tissue, and when the snot and the tears cleared, I saw the looks on their faces. It was concern but not patronising. It was 'you're here and that's half the battle but we're not going to fool you – this won't be easy'.

But, above all, it was understanding. We were all in this room because someone we loved was an addict. And although understanding was not something we met with often outside of that room, we were there because we knew our loved ones were not terrible people; they were worth saving. They were still the people we fell in love with, the child who once had so much joy and promise, the sibling we had pillow fights with.

I learned so much about empathy and kindness in that room. But there was no denying what I saw also scared me. From what I read on drug forums, addiction was formidable. Dr Shanahan described the urge as being so strong he knew of people who had clambered over the dead bodies of people who'd overdosed to get the drugs left behind.

Some of the people in my support group had been with their partners for years. I saw how much it had defined their life – that constant swing between recovery and relapse. The fear in their eyes   the anxious people it had turned them into.

I wanted to know if anyone had succeeded in making it work; if anyone's relationship had managed to survive. And all I found online were accounts of people dragged along the road of addiction with their partners, like their sleeves were caught in the window of a car and they were powerless to stop.

Perhaps this is testament to how much faith I had in Rob. Perhaps it is a sign of my own naivety or arrogance. But during the whole time I helped Rob through his recovery, especially in that first year, I was sure, so sure, we would be the exception to the rule.


Here's the thing I don't get about addiction: how, considering how widespread it is, we have managed to cock up treating it and being informed as to what it actually is.

The UK is described as the 'addiction capital of Europe'[4] and, although heroin use among the young has fallen, in the US there is something close to an epidemic. It has increased 63 per cent over the last eleven years. The number of women who use it has doubled, and there has been an increase in every demographic.[5]

It is telling that both countries employ a draconian approach to controlled drugs and addiction – a sentiment echoed by Dr Shanahan – and it is all too easy to draw parallels between their drug policies and ongoing failures to properly tackle a growing drug dependency crisis.

The general consensus is that drug addiction is bad, and people who are drug addicts are bad, and when someone who is a drug addict commits a crime, it is almost always framed in terms of their addiction.

Comprehending the nature of addiction is the first problem for a lot of people. Most of us have trouble understanding why someone doesn't simply stop.

'It's the craving and urge to use, following the loss of the substance,' said Dr Shanahan. 'It's not just an urge for chocolate or coffee. You can begin to understand it if you even look at smokers who cannot wait to get to their first, second or third cigarette. The average smoker takes seven attempts to give up cigarettes and we're looking at a legal substance.

'So the power of that feeling is magnified about twenty or thirty times with opiates. And therefore, if you take that from somebody, the loss to the body, the brain, the psyche, is unbearable. There is such an emptiness. They get sick as their body is withdrawing.

'And even if you show them the damage they are causing and get them into a nice [facility], that urge remains in place. So what you really need is a patient with time and interest, and a well-supported detox. But first you've got to make a proper diagnosis – what is going on with the person? Are they full of shame and guilt?

'That needs to be figured out before you go anywhere near "you're a naughty person, you must stop using, we don't like it".'

Most people's assumption about becoming an addict is that it takes either a single hit or using a drug several times, one or other of those two scenarios. But the truth is much more complex than that, and until we start having honest conversations about it at every level, it will be very difficult to reduce the number of users.

The journalist Johann Hari, who saw his career derailed by allegations of plagiarism in 2011, subsequently spent three years of his life understanding addiction and the war on drugs and has some insightful views on the subject.[6] He explains that while chemical 'hooks' are undoubtedly part of what keeps the person using the drug, it is not necessarily the whole story. He cites patients who go in for surgery and end up on morphine, but then do not go on to become morphine addicts once they leave.

After Rob told me about his addiction, he started to open up and talked honestly about his pattern of using. I always thought the emphasis was on withdrawal but, actually, the much bigger battle came after the drug was out of his system. The problem, he said, wasn't withdrawing, it was staying clean. It was all of those chickens come home to roost – the realisation of what he had done, the lies, the shame.

In a letter he wrote to his doctor asking for prescription drugs to get him through another relapse, he wrote:

What I've got myself into is a rolling, absolutely rubbish addiction, where – from the first incident, where a combination of self-isolation, arrogance, the worst bout of depression I've ever experienced occurred – I do a minimal amount of gear, breeze through the next 48–72 hours, until in fact I'm over the worst of the physical withdrawal.

However, it is at this point (and this is like clockwork) that the first, and probably worst, bout of clucking occurs, and while I intellectually and practically know why I need to get through to the other side without using, I become such a wreck, so quickly, and am overcome by hopelessness and all the other tricks my addiction can throw at me, that I use a tiny bit to get me through what feels like an eternity of misery every second. And so the pattern repeats itself.

Men are more likely to abuse drugs and alcohol than women. I wonder if this is due to an inability to articulate the need for help, coupled with short-term fixes to keep up appearances.

I spoke to Mr B, a well-vetted, anonymous contact who works with, for and around policy regarding mental health in the government. He said: 'When things are difficult for men, they seek solace in behaviours that enable them to escape. Those behaviours are categorised as an addiction.

'An addiction is where you get a buzz out of pursuing something that changes the chemistry in your brain, which makes you high or numb or makes you forget your problems. And if you have layers upon layers of things that trouble you, you will seek solace in escape. That escape becomes something you go back to in times of stress or times of "fuck it, it may be an addiction, but I enjoy it". And what follows is shame and guilt, or "I don't fit in".

'Then you get locked in this bubble of "you can't deal with it, but you can't confess to it". Because you know if you confess to it, you will feel the shame of others, and the criticism and rejection of others, which you want to stop because you know that might lead you back to that addiction. So it's a cycle.'

It may also go some way to explaining why more men kill themselves than women, as is the case in the UK. In his book *Cry of Pain: Understanding Suicide and the Suicidal Mind*, Prof. Williams says: 'Alcohol and substance abuse present major risk factors for suicide ... The prevalence of alcohol and drug abuse increases steadily from the age of fifteen until about forty-five, after which it declines.' Interestingly, this is also roughly the main age demographic for male suicides in the UK – the biggest killer of men under forty-five.

He continues:

The number of years somebody who completes suicide has typically been abusing alcohol is between twenty and twenty-five.

This may be because, as the alcoholism progresses, it erodes those factors known to protect against suicide:

first, it destroys social supports; second, it destroys intellectual function through brain damage ... third, chronic alcoholism reduces personal control and increases helplessness. Studies show that alcohol and drug abuse are most lethal when they occur alongside depression.

This tells us that an addict's journey is so much more complicated than we can imagine.

Like all addicts, Rob had long stopped having fun with drugs. And though the reasons why a person becomes an addict may be wide and varied, they are almost certainly taking drugs as a coping mechanism to deal with things that are too hard and too painful. And the longer the addiction goes on, the more that person becomes entrenched in drug use to cope with the shame of being an addict.

'Most people want to get away from these drugs,' Dr Shanahan told me, 'and the question is: why do [these] people want to stay on them?'

He believes that harmonisation – the word used to describe methadone treatment – can work, and the danger is when you have a government that believes it cannot.

'I think we are going to miss the people who simply cannot get off drugs and cannot stop using. There is no point pushing these people into abstinence on the basis that using methadone is simply parking them on it for life.

'My view on that is, so what? If people are alive and safe

and are given opportunities to get off it if they want to, I think it's perfectly reasonable to offer that structure. And some people need it. The Dutch, Germans and Swiss have all found success with it.'

So why on earth does any government assume that wagging a finger and demanding absolute abstinence would work? Especially seeing as it never, ever has in the history of the world.

In fact, Hari's theory – with which I partly agree – is that the way to tackle addiction is through human connection. Integration into society rather than penning them in a 'them and us' cage. Contrary to abstinence policies, evidence for the success of an integrated drugs strategy is overwhelming, showing how connecting with, rather than shunning, addicts can reduce deaths and crime.

The greatest travesty, however, is that when experts do advise the government or call for decriminalisation, they are fobbed off. In 2016, two of the major public health bodies in the UK – the Royal Society for Public Health and the Faculty of Public Health – called for the decriminalisation of drugs, saying the government's policies had failed.[7]

The government denied this, and claimed that drug dependency had dropped. So this means that the machine with the power to change drugs policy is ignoring the advice of two huge, well-respected and knowledgeable bodies about a problem that affects thousands of people in the UK, not to mention the thousands of loved ones around them.

It isn't just that the government – and this isn't political because it is an attitude that has cut across the major national parties for decades – is not listening to the experts who know what they are talking about, but nor does it look to other countries who have successfully managed to implement decriminalisation.

'Nearly fifteen years ago, Portugal had one of the worst drug problems in Europe, with 1 per cent of the population addicted to heroin,' wrote Hari.

'They had tried a drug war, and the problem just kept getting worse. So they decided to do something radically different. They resolved to decriminalise all drugs, and transfer all the money they used to spend on arresting and jailing drug addicts, and spend it instead on reconnecting them – to their own feelings, and to the wider society.'[8]

He has also written about Switzerland, which over ten years ago had a heroin epidemic similar to the one going on in the States at the moment. 'Under a visionary president – Ruth Dreifuss – they decided to try an experiment. If you are a heroin addict, you are assigned to a clinic, and you are given your heroin there, for free, where you use it supervised by a doctor or nurse. You are given support to turn your life around, and find a job, and housing.

'The result? Nobody has died of an overdose on legal heroin – literally nobody. Street crime fell significantly. The heroin epidemic ended. Most legal heroin users choose to reduce their dose and come off the program over time, because as they find work, and no longer feel stigmatised, they want to be present in their lives again.'

We use language to shame users, because we feel that they are persisting in their unhealthy lifestyle because they aren't aware of the impact they are having on other people. That they don't feel *bad enough* to stop.

How fucking laughable this is. How fucking sad that most of us, including myself, could think that *this* was the way to get results, rather than kindness and empathy.

Loneliness is such a huge driver of what compels someone to abuse drugs, yet instead of bothering to find this out, we and the powers that be decide that what they need is to be told clearly, in no uncertain terms, that until they fix themselves they are not allowed back into society.

Imagine the *shame* this causes a person. How can they ever hope to get the right kind of help, when everything is such a desperate race to wallpaper over the cracks so that they can rejoin the inner circle as quickly as possible?

For men, shame can be deadly. In Rob's case, it was deadly. When I spoke to Jane, who used to run the male suicide prevention charity CALM, she said: 'There is no give because there is no permission for give. Either you're a proper man or you're not.

'So things like shame, embarrassment, guilt – failure to be a proper man is the ultimate disgrace for them. I often think what that must be like. Here you are, God's chosen one. You're supposed to do everything. Be responsible for everyone around you.'

Rob should have gone on methadone but what with him not being a child, I couldn't force him to do it. His main reason for not wanting to go on it was because he felt it was shameful. The flipside to trying to redeem himself from feeling shameful was to try to fix it himself – something that continuously exasperated Prue and me.

This uncompromising sense of belief, the rigidity of 'I can sort it out', can be deadly. Prof. Williams refers to it as part of the similarity between depression and addiction.

'The difference between people who have an addiction and don't get into trouble with it, and people who have addiction and do get into trouble is the fixity of the belief. Say it's a gambling addiction. Some people would say, "I'm just doing it for fun", other people would say, "I've got a system and that system will work despite all the evidence to the contrary. My system will get me out of trouble." Even if – in the case of gambling – they are in huge debt. They don't look at the actuality of the evidence.

'Depression is very much like that in a way, in that you have a fixed belief that "I can't do anything about this pain, and no one else can do anything about this pain ever". And when you understand the fixity – the way in which that belief is so stuck in place – then it enables you to understand how desperate it all is.'

Rob was the product of a middle-class family, someone who had ticked the boxes he was expected to since birth – job, house, wife – who had then been faced with the fact that he had depression, which he had tried to self-medicate since the age of fifteen.

He had to accept that this had now turned him into an addict. He also had to accept the reality of what his behaviour had done to our marriage. And then he had to enter the system to get a heavily controlled drug, the process of which was more humiliating than calling up a drug dealer.

Of course, there are some people who abuse the system. Who save it up or sell it on. But there are also a lot of people who don't and who need the stability that a methadone or Subutex replacement therapy provides. Contrary to what anti-drugs politicians say, methadone isn't quite the easy drugs fix they assume it to be. You don't simply pick it up like a box of macaroons and skip merrily home.

We looked into it. You have to notify the DVLA because it affects the conditions of your driving licence. In fact, the DVLA's attitude to it is indicative of the unbelievably cack-handed attitude to methadone treatment generally, in that it categorises it as a 'disability'.

You can get a permit to take your methadone script on holiday but it applies only to UK customs control. It states very clearly: 'Clients should be aware that it has no legal status outside the UK.' So no holidays abroad, unless you like being in foreign prisons.

And you may be thinking, *Oh poor widdle babies can't go on holiday*, but we were trying our hardest to keep up appearances with our families. How could we explain – with relatives in New Zealand and India – that we couldn't go on family holidays, ever, without telling them the truth?

You also have to go on an 'Addicts Index', presumably so doctors can monitor who is using what drug and when. You're told it doesn't affect your ability to get a job, but that's putting a lot of trust in a system that doesn't trust you.

When you pick up your script from a chemist, they may just say loudly in front of other customers, 'Here's your methadone.' If you're agitated that day – which could be because your bus was late or you had a shit day at work – they may make you take it in front of them, so they know you aren't hoarding it. I mean, seriously, why not make people wear a sandwich board with 'JUNKIE' on the front of it before they go in, you know, in the hope that their shame might put someone off using?

The irony of how people can access controlled drugs safely in the UK and US is that every step ensures they are marked out as different, outside the norms of society, when it's more than likely that an addict started using because they didn't feel like they fitted into the society they were expected to serve and obey.

In support groups, you find out the cost addiction exacts on a life.

We are taught from a young age that the addict is unclean; a creature to be shunned, to be treated as a horror story, as an example to all good girls and boys so that they never, ever go down that path. And you, as the spouse, fight against making your own judgements every damn day. It takes all your will not to assume that your supposedly clean partner isn't using that extra five minutes in the bathroom to get high. Or there genuinely *was* traffic when they went out to the supermarket and that's why they were late.

I wasn't just dealing with judgement from the government. I was dealing with the devastating loneliness that comes from not being able to tell people that your loved one is an addict. Because how could I expect them to react with anything less than disgust when that would have been my reaction, if life had been different?

So, there was grief for my old life, loneliness in my new life; and all the time, every minute of every day apart from when I lay in bed with Rob and we talked and held each other, my life was fake.

No part of my life was free from the cover-up, especially work. The day after I found out Rob was an addict, I called my boss and said my husband was sick, he'd be in and out of hospital and I'd need some flexibility in my working hours. I'm fairly sure they all assumed he had cancer. I didn't correct them.

When you're having a bad day and your stomach is in knots because you can't get hold of your loved one on the phone, or they call you up and ask you to transfer some money because *that payment didn't arrive on time*, or the GP apparently didn't have time to do a drugs test that morning, you cannot tell people at work the truth. You can't explain why your colleagues need to be kinder to you on a certain morning, or why you need to work from home occasionally to make sure you don't find your husband swinging from his bedroom door. The silence around addiction gags you. It makes you live a double life that you didn't want in the first place.

While I tried to keep my anger from Rob, I found it impossible at times to reconcile the man I loved with the candy floss of lies he had wrapped around us both. In the search for Rob's absolution, I asked Dr Shanahan what he thought.

'You have to ask yourself, what is the common denominator to all of these problems? And if it's the drug use, then that's the link. Because there won't be any lying if it's about other things not related to getting to the drug.'

I thought of when Rob had lied – the night-time walks with Daisy, the odd explanations about money, the insomnia.

'They are not untruthful and dishonest people, they just want heroin,' said Dr Shanahan. 'And therefore you have to ask yourself, why are we not giving it to them? Why are we making it so difficult for these people and blocking them, rather than giving them a few months or years of stability so they can stop lying? Then they can actually build a life, so they can say, "I feel better, can I try at redemption now?"'

While his words made me feel better, they also filled me with such sadness that this was not a path we took for Rob.

I have no doubt there are sections of society – big

sections – that believe addicts are a waste of space. That if indeed they are killing themselves, either through an overdose or suicide, then it's nature's way of thinning out a segment of the population that can't function as well as others.

But if you're going down that route, then let's remove the services that save lives from cancer. Let's unplug the ventilators and stop putting stents into people's hearts. Let's remove therapists, doctors, nurses – anyone who tries to heal someone who is sick or isn't able to get by without help from other people. Let's see how many lives that affects, whether those human beings and their families will mind.

Addicts can lie, they can let us down in the most terrible of ways. They cause chaos unlike any other. Some of them steal. They break our hearts and our trust. But we don't question the moral ethics of someone with a physical illness as a reason for whether they can have treatment.

We don't ask if they were naughty or nice, before deciding if they are worth saving.

Remembrance can be abstract and literal at the same time. Abstract because a mere fragment can set off a deep grief pinpointing to the sharp sensation of loss. Literal such as seeing a photo or coming across a pair of their socks.

Cemeteries are very literal places for remembrance.

Before Rob passed away, apart from grandparents who had reached the natural end of their lives, no one close to me had died.

Looking back on it, I was lucky. I know people who have prematurely lost parents, nieces, nephews, best friends, and it shaped the rest of their lives.

When I was in New Zealand just after Rob died, we visited the cemetery to pick a plot. What I wasn't prepared for was this huge expanse of greenery, the sense of calm.

We buried him in a plot in full view of the sun, and the edge dips into a valley of water where yachts bob in the distance.

Although I have talked to him constantly since he passed, whispered into the line where the sea meets the shore, talked out loud across moors, along rivers, by duck ponds, spoken into the megaphone of clouds funnelling above my head, this is the anchor and root of where he is.

I have longed for this place, yearned to sit beside him, but I am also terrified of what it may unplug emotionally. Will I start wailing and lose control?

*The first time I visit the cemetery after he was buried nine months before, I take Prue with me. She gives me time alone to sit by him. And I cry. Not huge gulps, but I cry a little bit. I place my hand on the ground and try to reach out to his body lying far down below.*

*It seems wrong there is sunshine. That the grass has grown. That cicadas – the sound of summer in my ears – are humming while he will never speak again.*

*The importance of a grave, I realise in that moment, is it winches you back to reality when your mind tries to tell you this could not possibly have happened. That this man, whose hands once held your waist, whose lips kissed your own, who was the greatest love of your life, is now lying below your feet. Nature knows this to be true because grass has started to grow over him like a blanket.*

*But he is not asleep, he is gone. There is an expectation to feel him there, to feel something tangible and filled with comfort, and the absence of that is cold and empty.*

*When I return to the cemetery alone, a few days later, it is completely different. John Denver comes on the radio, 'Rocky Mountain High', a song Rob loved. It's warm and in the distance I can hear 'Amazing Grace' being played on bagpipes at a funeral nearby.*

*I realise Rob isn't his body; he is the songs he loved, the plants he photographed and the letters he wrote to all of us. And rather than an absence at his grave, I feel Rob pouring in.*

*I took vows, and while his life was not mine, it was half*

*of mine and I promised to be there for him in sickness and in health.*

I'm sorry, *I whisper.*

*I say it like a rosary prayer, over and over.*

I'm sorry, I'm so sorry, Bobbie, I'm so sorry.

*I ask him for forgiveness. I tell him how much I miss him, the smell of his hair, the sound of his voice.*

*As I sit in this swell of new grief, I think about how all of those people will feel when they see the coffin being lowered into the earth. How it will stay chiselled into their memories for years to come, each second of that moment hammered in stone, blood and pain.*

# Chapter Eight

**Narcotics Anonymous Chapter Meeting**
**Date: January 2015**

Robert Owen Bell was the guest speaker:

People come to Narcotics Anonymous in all kinds of states and often full of preconceptions – 'It was wrapped up in my head with the Salvation Army,' one addict tells the room to laughter, 'I expected tambourines and God-botherers.'

I came into my first meeting three days clean after a quarter century of heavy drug and alcohol use, culminating in a ten-year relationship with heroin that began as a flirtation, became a love affair and ended in four years lost to an addiction that stripped me of everything I valued in and outside of myself, still dope-sick, clucking, cursing the cold that had fallen on the city the day I'd gone into withdrawal.

There were no tambourines. Smiles, yes. Hugs from strangers, yes. A commonality of experience that helped draw me out of the nightmare my life had become, yes.

Hope for those lost to hopelessness, definitely.

I struggle with aspects of the NA programme and probably always will. However, rather than reading like a tract, the philosophy of the 'fellowship of NA' sounds more like a political manifesto from the turn of the last century.

'A non-profit fellowship or society of men and women for whom drugs had become a major problem', NA is made up of 'recovering addicts who meet regularly to help each other stay clean'.

'Anyone may join us, regardless of age, race, sexual identity, creed, religion, or lack of religion,' it continues. 'The newcomer is the most important person at any meeting, because we can only keep what we have by giving it away. We have learned from our group experience that those who keep coming to our meetings regularly stay clean.'

Meetings begin with a few simple readings steeped in an honesty most addicts feel they have lost from their lives forever: 'Who is an addict? Most of us do not have to think twice about this question. We know! Our whole life and thinking was centred on drugs in one form or another – the getting and using and finding ways and means to get more. We lived to use and used to live. Very simply, an addict is a man or woman whose life is controlled by drugs. We are people in the grip of a continuing and progressive illness whose ends are always the same: jails, institutions, and death.'

This statement both resonates and rankles. I struggle to agree with the idea of my addiction as an 'illness'. Is this the last of my pride? Or am I turning my back on an easy excuse?

Having professed the non-religious nature of NA, I'm going to ruin it with a biblical metaphor. Growing up in a devoutly Christian household, the passage in the New Testament that meant the most to me was Jesus, a man, alone and about to die, crying out on the Cross, 'My God, why have you forsaken me?'

Drug addicts don't live in Hell, that bustling metropolis of souls united in torment, but hang helpless on a lonely hill, facing a tomorrow over which they have lost control, of more lies, shame, betrayal; a tomorrow of abasing themselves once more before a God whose only currency is death, but which cannot be denied or abandoned without great suffering.

Drugs strip the addict of everything he or she values, both within and without.

NA addicts are reminded why they are in the rooms: 'Before coming to the fellowship of NA, we could not manage our own lives. We could not live and enjoy life as other people do. We had to have something different and we thought we had found it in drugs. We placed their use ahead of the welfare of our families, our wives, husbands and our children. We had to have drugs at all costs. We did many people great harm, but most of all we harmed ourselves. Through our inability to accept personal responsibilities we were actually creating our own problems. We seemed to be incapable of facing life on its own terms.

'Most of us realised that in our addiction we were slowly committing suicide, but addiction is such a cunning enemy of life that we had lost the power to do anything about it. Many of us ended up in jail, or sought help through medicine, religion and psychiatry. None of these methods was sufficient for us. Our disease always resurfaced or continued to progress until, in desperation, we sought help from each other in Narcotics Anonymous.'

Addicts lose their partners, children, jobs and homes, alienate the family and friends they steal from to support their habits, or push away as they become increasingly isolated. They disappear from social circles in an attempt to hide their problem, consumed by shame, embarrassed by their helplessness.

I was lucky in still having a roof over my head and a loving wife willing to support me through recovery, but most addicts come into the room having hit rock bottom. Early on, I heard the story of a man who had drifted into London from the North with a bag of crack cocaine and a wad of cash in his pocket.

He woke in a Euston cemetery with nothing and was soon living on the streets, begging to survive, hopelessly addicted to alcohol and drugs. He was visibly deteriorating, and a woman staffing the day centre where he sometimes showered and grabbed a cup of tea offered to get him into rehab – but there was a catch: he had to enter rehab clean.

It was January, and New Year's resolutions meant detox centres were full to bursting, but having hit rock bottom he found a new determination and holed up with his sleeping bag (his only possession) out the back of the local Iceland.

'I detoxed behind Iceland in the middle of the coldest winter of my life,' he says. 'And a couple of days in, the cops who usually moved me on were buying me pasties and bottles of water, and the manager and his staff were cheering me on – he's gone three days! Four!'

He left behind the cold of January 1991 to enter rehab and has been clean since. Now that took guts. And heart. In rehab he joined NA, and over a decade later still attends meetings – not just for himself but to help other addicts. Remember: 'We can only keep what we have by giving it away.'

By the end of my heroin addiction, intimacy was almost completely lost to me. I spoke to no one but the parasitic dealers who kept me in gear; I snuck into bed hours after my wife to lie rigid beside her, consumed by guilt and shame, cowering behind the tissue of lies that hid my addiction.

My friends were gone; everyone I knew I had made a stranger.

But in the rooms my fellow addicts offered smiles, hugs, laughter, profanity, understanding, acceptance, as much support – or space – as I needed, a text message, a sugary tea and a chocolate biscuit.

And I soaked that empathy up, a thirsty man in the desert stumbling into an oasis. I had been alone for so long, in my head and heart, isolated, lost, kneeling helpless before my addiction every morning.

In NA I found help I could grasp, made tangible in the story I share with the other addicts in the rooms and the love given freely by those who had once thought love was lost from their life to those who have lost their belief they deserve love.

NA meetings also begin 'with a moment of silence, to think of all addicts still suffering, both in and outside of these rooms'.

So to all those addicts (especially those worried they're going to be God-bothered into submission) still suffering in the cold, I can only say *come inside.*

# Chapter Nine

'What came first,' asked Rob's psychiatrist, 'the addiction or the depression?'

We were sitting in the Priory, in The Doctor's expensive office, drinking rapidly cooling tea. It was a rhetorical question.

As we waited in the natural pause that followed, I heard Rob pacing outside while we had this private chat. Wondering what his doctor would tell me. Wondering if I would leave him, when I finally knew the true extent of it all.

After Rob told me the truth about his addiction, I agreed to stay with him and work through it on one condition. If he relapsed or felt close to relapsing, he would tell me and we would get help. The worst thing, I said, was being lied to.

'I love you, but my parents didn't raise me to be an idiot,' I said.

In the nine months following that conversation, Rob relapsed twice. Once on heroin, once on alcohol. Both times had been surrounded yet again by layer upon layer of lies; he had allowed weeks to pass, weeks where I questioned my own sanity, where I questioned him, before he finally owned up.

Although by now I knew the signs – lack of sleep, a reluctance to come to bed at the same time as me, borrowing money and loss of appetite – somehow he had still managed to hoodwink me. He traded on excuses and the trust I had in him, what little was left of it.

Why didn't I leave him? Why didn't I just say no, put my foot down and demand utter compliance?

Because I was human and I had feelings. I wasn't a doctor; I wasn't dealing with a patient. Because what kind of marriage was it if I became the disciplinarian and treated him like a child?

Rob was a human being, a difficult, obstinate, often aggravating human being, but nonetheless an adult who deserved dignity, and, like other people struggling with a dual diagnosis of mental illness and addiction, he needed it more than most.

I don't know how I knew this but I did: the reason why Rob had come to this point was because he believed he wasn't worth anything. The most important thing I could do for him was to help restore his humanity.

While I'm painfully aware how Rob's battle with

addiction ended, I asked Dr Shanahan if he noticed any commonalities in people who managed to stay clean for years. He said that 'the insulation of hope was very important to people'.

'The feeling that something better *was* possible. The maintenance of friendships, however thin and tenuous they were. Just someone who continued to trust and believe in them a little bit. Just believing, as I do, that if there is life, there's hope.'

I don't think people realise how hard it is when you are trying to decipher genuine cause from excuses, when your relationship is lost in a moral miasma of grey and half-truths. It's not as simple as shutting the door, kicking them out.

When you don't know the truth, when all you are going on is a bellyful of paranoia and anxiety, your love for the other person holds you hostage.

The first time he relapsed, he managed a month before confessing. I couldn't fathom how, despite forgiving him and helping him through recovery, despite the very high cost I paid in terms of all my relationships, especially my parents, he had reverted to lying again.

'Does our marriage really mean that little to you?' I asked. 'Do you seriously not give a fuck about how hard this is for me?'

He tried to explain that it had nothing to do with us, and that it had everything to do with his own struggle with addiction.

Shortly afterwards, in a letter to his doctor that I saw without him knowing, he said: 'I want to be clean, for good. I want it more than I've ever wanted anything in my life, and I know I can do it. I did it towards the end of last year, and I have complete faith in myself that I can do it again, and without it ending in a relapse as it has this time.'

Although I was fed up and felt like I'd heard it all before, I was sure he could do it.

I made him promise again.

With blue eyes big and full of fear that he would lose me, he swore he wouldn't ever touch drugs again. That he knew, that he'd learned, that he would not mess this up. 'I love you,' he said. 'You are the most important thing to me. Please, honey, please give me another chance.'

We began recovery again the next day. Two days of silence and being sick in the spare room that doubled up as his office, and then after a time I would hear music coming from his room again. When Rob was back in active addiction, you knew because he wouldn't play music.

When he was well, he'd sit at his computer and play Billy Bragg, the Carpenters, Slayer, Turbonegro, The Specials, Townes Van Zandt, Gil Scott-Heron and his favourite at that time, Nekrogoblikon, a 'melodic death metal' band whose material centred mainly around goblins and whose mascot was a guy wearing a goblin suit called John Goblikon.

I have ears that stick out, and when I scraped my hair back, he'd look lovingly at me and say: 'Aw, baby, you look just like a goblin.'

'How'd you like my goblin foot up your ass?' I'd reply with a glare.

In the mornings, he'd make a strong coffee with four sugars, light up a cigarette and stick something fast and loud on. In the afternoons he'd sing along to Karen Carpenter and make Daisy's paws dance in time to the music. The evenings were mainly James Taylor, a musician who'd had his own battles with drugs and had emerged clean and sober as this wonderfully kind, worldly man. I think Rob saw hope in that for himself.

We were still renting, and decided to move to the more sedate, leafy streets of Middlesex. South London was too druggy and there were too many bad memories. But in between our house move, Rob underwent the second major relapse since his proper attempt at recovery in 2014. This time on alcohol, which meant the downward spiral was far quicker and more destructive.

It started very innocuously. A couple of beers when we were in India in April for a cousin's wedding, back when I didn't know that recovery meant no drugs whatsoever, including alcohol.

Three months later, we then moved far away from the drug

dealers in Streatham to quiet, suburban Hampton where we didn't know anyone, and visited our local pub as part of our introduction to the area. Then I noticed that Rob went to the same pub the next day. And the next day. He would have a couple of beers every evening.

A week went by, and I voiced my concern. I could see the patterns of addiction returning. The excuses: 'It's sunny'; the bargaining: 'It's only one'; and eventually the lying: bank statements revealed he had been to the off-licence every night and somehow had managed to conceal it.

When Rob died, I rescued as many of his voicemails as I could. I wanted to remember his voice, turn it over on my tongue like a chocolate, feel it pass through my ears and pour that remembrance into myself.

But there is one that I hate because it is so nonchalant. It is the perfect example of how he manipulated my concern to make it seem dramatic, unwarranted, when he was disguising his substance abuse.

He left the message for me while I was on a train back home to Hampton, a commute I hated because the trains only ran every half an hour, and it seemed to take forever to get home. In the voicemail, he said he was in the pub and knew I'd be furious and 'overreact', but that I didn't have anything to worry about and he didn't want to fight.

It was at this time that I would have one of the worst nights of my life with Rob.

It starts with him spending most of the night playing music

and clattering around loudly. When I wake up, tetchy from a night of bad sleep, I come downstairs to find him sprawled on the floor next to the dog. I think he's asleep, but he isn't, he's passed out drunk.

I don't know this yet.

I see the car has been parked haphazardly outside the house; the windows rolled down. I am late for my train; I don't understand what I'm seeing.

I yell at Rob to wake up, but he doesn't. I'm pissed off. Fed up. But I've got to get to work. We live in a safe neighbourhood, the car will be fine.

I've just been promoted so work is intense. It's a long day, and while on my way home, sweating on the hot train, I get a phone call. It's Rob and I can't understand what he's saying. At first I think it's a bad connection then I realise he can't actually talk.

'Are you drunk?' I yell incredulously.

He's so drunk he can't even answer. The temperature of my skin feels like the surface of the sun. I am so angry and I feel myself welling up but I can't cry, I won't cry on this train full of goddamn suburban commuters travelling towards their wonderfully sedate picket-fence lives.

I sit rigid, with my mask on, for the longest forty-minute journey in the history of Poorna.

When I get home, he can't stand. He becomes belligerent because I won't talk to him. I won't talk to him because he is swaying and his eyes are rolling in his head. I feel disgusted.

I want this man as far from me as possible. This isn't the person I know. The person who placed a ring on my finger promising to honour and cherish me wouldn't put me in this horror show.

He's a fucking stranger; he's breaking my heart.

He follows me into the kitchen. On some level, through the fog, he knows something is wrong but can't seem to work out why I'm so angry.

I ignore him. While I'm chopping up vegetables he loses his balance and his face smacks down hard on the tiled floor. I swear I hear a crack. That gets my attention. I fight the urge to cry. I go over to him as he lies on the floor.

He is heavy. He is big and I'm not strong, so I can't lift him up properly. I've never been more scared for him, for me, and for us. Finally, he gets up.

He tells me he has been drinking in secret for two weeks. He tells me he has been self-harming and shows me cigarette burns pressed into his skin. I want to throw up. I want to leave, run as far as I can from him but I can't. I can't leave him alone; my love becomes a chain that binds our feet together.

I'm so exhausted and I need to sleep. He doesn't understand why he can't come into the bedroom. Rob hates it when we don't sleep in the same bed together, which I've only made him do once in our relationship when he was detoxing. He becomes upset but I keep the door closed and he doesn't come in.

Eventually, he falls asleep outside the door.

I wake up in the morning and I call work. 'There's been an emergency,' I say flatly.

Rob wakes up at the sound of my voice, now sober. I ignore him while I get ready.

'Honey, please talk to me.'

I look at him. This is probably the first time I've seen him. I mean, properly *seen* him. I've always known about the beauty of him, but, finally, I have seen the destruction. It has looked me in the eye, it has burned itself onto his flesh, and it is so raw, so much older and more powerful than me. It scares me.

Now that he is sober he looks like my husband again. But I'm afraid of my anger, and I cannot be in the same house as him. I don't want him to harm himself while I am away. The danger of suicide hangs in the room like the stench of an abattoir, death flapping its wings like a moth in the darkness, worms wriggling in the dank earth.

I can taste the remorse in the air, bitter and full of self-hatred. I know that a hangover and a depressive slump await him. But I need space to think.

'I'm going to my sister's. I will talk to you when I get back.'

'Are you leaving me?'

'No. I'll be back in the evening.'

I get in my car and I drive to Priya's house in Brighton. For the first time since we married, I start to doubt whether

I can do this. Rob's problems are so great they seem beyond me. How can I stop someone who is steadily destroying himself?

I knew we wouldn't have a normal life like other couples but I tried everything.

I sold myself into debt to help him.

I have walled my friends off from the truth of my life, and I cannot tell my parents, the two people I love most in the world aside from Rob, who have worked so hard to keep me safe, whose kindness and generosity I don't deserve, who would go to the ends of the earth for me. I have let them down; this is not the daughter they raised. I disgust myself. I don't know what I did to deserve this, or where I went wrong.

I hate the person I am turning into. Controlling, paranoid, upset. Permanently broke, permanently angry, a liar, carrying the entire weight of our marriage.

Love is not enough, I realise for the first time. It should be, but it isn't. We need proper help.

In two days, Rob will voluntarily enter a psychiatric hospital as an in-patient for the first time in his life.


The Doctor's office was not as clinical as I thought it would be. I imagined a white cube, but it was more like a living room in the suburbs.

The outside of the Priory, when you drive up, resembles a hotel. A white-iced wedding cake of a building with spiralling turrets and manicured gardens. A week's stay costs £4,000, so presumably all of this is to make mental illness more palatable.

When I dropped Rob off, my anger had distilled into concern and protectiveness. I was relieved we had managed to get private care through my insurance, but I still wanted to know he was in a safe place.

My first awareness of a psychiatric hospital was in Bangalore when I was a child. It was a place called Nimhans. Back then we didn't know it stood for the National Institute of Mental Health and Neuroscience.

Nimhans became a colloquialism when I was a kid; it was shorthand for crazy. 'Don't be a loony or you'll get sent to Nimhans' is what we'd say when someone did something bad, silly or unreasonable. It was a place for people who raved constantly, who needed to be strapped down – the stereotypical depictions of psych wards in movies.

If you did something odd, you'd be asked if you'd just escaped from Nimhans. If you wanted to discredit someone, you'd suggest they be carted off to Nimhans.

Our warped view of mental health begins as children, and I don't know anyone, except Mr B, who has a healthy understanding of mental illness or the hospitals that treat such people. He did because his parents worked and lived in the grounds of a psychiatric hospital.

'My take comes from being around what the rest of society calls extremely damaged people who need to be removed, treated, fixed or forgotten about. And I only ever saw the humanity in them. What we've categorised as mental illness has been our way of categorising them as "Others".'

At the Priory, I wasn't prepared for how nice it seemed. But I still wanted to double-check everything. I wanted to see his room, which looked like any you'd get in a four-star hotel.

'This place looks so fancy,' I marvelled when I came for my first visit.

'Don't be fooled,' Rob said. 'It's still a hospital.' I was reminded of that when we talked on the phone and every fifteen minutes we'd be interrupted by someone conducting suicide checks.

'I don't want to sound facetious,' he said, 'but the other patients and I were talking, and if someone really wanted to kill themselves, they'd be able to do it within fifteen minutes.'

A group of people sitting around having a conversation about how quickly they could kill themselves? It sounded fucking horrible but I didn't say so.

Rob spent two weeks in the Priory, and he seemed to make rapid progress. He appeared driven and, for once, not blasé about his care. Perhaps this was because I had given him an ultimatum. Either he got proper treatment and we had a marriage where we both made the effort 50:50, or I would call it quits and leave.

It was the push he needed. Rather than going into his

sessions with a swagger that said he knew better, he engaged with other people. He was talkative, which was a relief, after months of silence. He told me about the therapy groups, he went to mindfulness sessions; he told me what he'd learned about himself and, for the first time in years, he started going to the gym in the hospital.

Although he had been visiting The Doctor for a least a year before he went in, I believe this was the first proper, intensive care he had received in his entire life.

I made several visits. I popped Daisy in the car and sang to her on the way there to soothe her in the traffic; we spent time in the grounds while he chain-smoked. As Daisy snuffled around for balls hidden in the bushes, there was a steady procession of staff and other patients passing through to say hello. Somehow, he'd already made friends with everyone.

'Seriously, how do you do that?' I asked. He shrugged and pointed at a girl. 'See her?' he said. She looked like any other girl on the street in jeans and a loose cotton t-shirt.

'She's been here for eight months. Eight months.' We sat for a while in silence, but I knew he was wondering how long it would take for him to become well, and what would happen if he didn't.

When I spoke to his doctors, they all assured me he was making real progress and was engaging in sessions brilliantly. His main revelation, he told me on the phone one evening, was that he hadn't realised how lonely he had been. 'I think

I need to stop freelancing and start working in an office,' he said. 'I've just spent too much time in my own head. And I need to start communicating more.'

Hallelujah. It seemed like we might finally be about to have our life back.

Rob had the option of spending his third week as a daily outpatient, and he really wanted to come home, to me, to his books, cuddling Daisy, and to start a new life for himself. A few days before he was due to leave, The Doctor asked to see me.

I strolled in, thinking this would be just another reassurance that Rob was a superstar and was doing really well. I had never seen him so positive, full of energy, so committed to being clean.

Although I would grow to like The Doctor – and indeed respect him for his diligence, patience and accurate reading of the situation despite how challenging a patient Rob must have been – when I first met him he scared the living daylights out of me. It also impressed me how, despite having dealt with a lot of people like Rob, and often being faced with difficult odds, he still had hope for each of his patients and treated them with kindness.

'So, what came first? The depression or the addiction?' he asked. And, as if reading my thoughts, he fixed his gaze on me and said: 'We will never know.'

'But Poorna,' he continued, 'I can treat the depression. With the right medication, I can treat it. But I don't know if Rob really understands how much the addiction is also part of it. At the moment, he's in what we call the "pink cloud".

'When people are in the pink cloud, they do things like book holidays, go out more. And although they seem strong, that's actually when they are most vulnerable, and that's when they relapse.'

Rob and I had just been speaking about going to Jesse's wedding in the Isle of Wight. He seemed so certain that he'd be okay to do it but I was now starting to have doubts.

'He has to understand how strong his addiction problems are. And at the moment, he thinks most of it is depression. But he has a severe addiction problem that he's been dealing with for twenty-five years. The only way you are going to get through it is either a proper detox facility, or by him doing the ninety meetings in ninety days at NA, being actively involved in his sobriety every minute of the day, and continuing appointments here. But he has to be able to come out of it, or he will lose everything.'

I felt our life slipping away. It sounded like an impossible task. The confidence I felt at Rob's renewed sense of recovery was evaporating. The feeling of nausea returned. We couldn't send him to a detox facility. Mainly because we couldn't afford it and also because I still hadn't yet told my parents about his addiction – they thought he was in hospital because of his depression.

Dual diagnosis is extremely hard to treat, primarily because it is hard to disentangle the addiction from the mental illness. It is chicken and egg: do you have a drug addiction because you had mental illness and were trying to self-medicate, or do you have a mental illness as a result of the drugs you have taken?

I found a 2002 study that showed that 85 per cent of alcoholics had mental health problems, while among drug users it was 75 per cent. Dual diagnosis isn't a fringe issue but far more prevalent and complex than most people would imagine.

In Rob's case, I believe he had a mental illness that he tried to self-medicate with drug use. He was self-harming long before his substance use became abuse. But am I saying that because I'm still clinging onto old stigmas, and somehow mental illness seems more moral than addiction?

Or maybe the diagnosis doesn't matter. The biggest obstacle in Rob's way seemed to be his inability to ask for help, his insistence that he was right and could fix everything, as well as his own shame at being an addict and having a mental illness. A study in 2010 revealed that men had a much higher self-stigma against depression than women.

I looked up Tony Blair's old right-hand man Alastair Campbell, who now spends his time campaigning for better understanding about mental health. Much of this is driven by his own personal journey. As we sat outside a tiny café in London, I asked how he felt about being admitted to a psychiatric hospital after his breakdown.

'Some people who get admitted haven't made the judgement in their own mind that they want to do it. I was so bad – I remember lying in this hospital bed thinking, *Fucking hell, how has this happened?* and in my head I reached my own realisation that I had to sort this out.

'Whereas a lot of people when they get admitted think, *I'm not as bad as that guy, why am I here, this is a complete waste of time.* Or they might think, *You've put me here because you can't cope.* The patient has to reach their own judgement.'

I didn't know how much Rob hated being in the hospital. He always made out like he was glad to be there, and I suppose in a way he was, because he saw it as his second chance at our marriage. I don't know that he ever fully accepted or believed it was a second chance for himself.

But there was a difference between the Rob who went in, and the Rob who came out. The Rob who came out was the man I fell in love with five years before. He was determined, hopeful; scared but glad to have his mind back.

Jesse was one of the few friends to go and visit him. When I asked him how he'd found Rob, he said: 'It felt like a lot of things had been stripped away and he had his feet on the ground and was being honest with me.

'We talked about a lot of shit. I mean, especially about how lonely he felt. We talked about addiction. His plans going forward. It felt like he had so many plans. He felt sad – smaller than he usually was, but more real too. He felt relatable.'

When Rob came home, I was suspicious that this new version of him was another mask to fool me. But when I didn't see the resurgence of insomnia, sweating or unreliability, or strange behaviour with money, I began for the first time to hope we may have a chance.

Hampton is near a huge park called Bushy, a wilder expanse than nearby Richmond Park with its crowds of joggers in expensive Lycra and Old Money walking their pedigree dogs. Instead, Bushy has empty stretches of moor with golden grasses, deer that clomp through patches of trees and hidden puddles perfect for one Daisy Bell to barrel into and cover herself in mud. Where we lived was far removed from anyone we knew, so it allowed our world to become smaller and utterly about us.

We spent time walking, our favourite spot being the Water Garden, cascading sheets of water pooling into a large pond inspected regularly by ducks. To the left, a tiny stream crossed by a bridge, where we came across a secret dilapidated wooden house and tried to peer inside the slats. We found sticks for Daisy, and Rob would put my hand in his coat pocket when the weather turned nippy.

He came to bed with me at the same time every night. At first it was odd. I had grown so used to developing my own little survival mechanisms to fill the space where he wasn't that it felt strange to have him bounding into bed with me, wanting to talk about his day.

He brought me peppermint tea, and in exchange I'd let him have one of my fancy bedtime chocolates from Fortnum and Mason.

His newfound zeal for the gym meant we went together at the weekends again, an activity I was used to doing on my own. We also did something we had never done before except when on holiday: we went shopping, we got coffee together in the daytime, and just talked. We looked just like any other couple.

He started to look healthier; his skin became plumper, less drawn around the eyes. We took pictures for his new Twitter account because I offered to help him build up an online profile in an effort to get him new work.

I love these pictures. He looks hopeful, happy even.

Three months after he came out of hospital, we went to see James Taylor in concert at the Royal Albert Hall, and when he played 'Something in the Way She Moves', Rob pressed my hand and whispered: 'This song is about you, baby.'

We cried when he sang 'Carolina in My Mind', a song that marked some of the darkest moments of Rob's recovery, playing from his computer while he was stretched out on the bed trying to gather the pieces of his mind shattered after withdrawal.

Every Saturday started the same.

I'd taken to buying white sheets, and we'd wake up in our own little snow-coloured world, our arms around each other. If we decided to go to yoga, we'd be up at 8am and tripping over ourselves to get out of the door and to class on time.

If we didn't, we'd wake up around nine. We'd kiss each other, our bottom lips meeting at their fullest swell. Then we'd have the same conversation.

'So, what do you want to do today?' I'd ask.

'Let's go to the gym. We can go to Gosia's afterwards and have coffee.'

'Mmm. Shall we get some rolls and make sandwiches for lunch?'

'Yes, and a nap. Got to have an afternoon nap together.'

'What do you want to do in the evening?'

'Download a film, maybe. Make something flash for dinner?'

For months after Rob died, as I lay under the sheets alone, my grief swelled with each breath I took. It puffed into my pillows, it crawled under the nook of my arm and into my throat. I held on to it as tightly as it held on to me.

I would close my eyes and call that perfect morning back into existence. I would repeat these lines to myself over and over again, and pretend I was just waiting for him to come back to bed, holding the moment for as long as I could.

*

I have never been the maternal type.

That doesn't mean I don't want kids, but the only person I ever wanted kids with was Rob. It was part of a bigger story than just wanting to procreate. It was about the life we were building together, pouring ourselves into a vessel to create the perfect mix of the two of us.

You know, like when you mix your own paint at the hardware store but presumably more rewarding.

When Rob and I first started talking about children, roughly two months into our relationship, I knew how much he wanted them, and I surprised myself by wanting them as much as he did. We pictured a boy and a girl, both with skin the colour of a cappuccino, crazy curly hair; green eyes like mine, long legs and strong bodies like him.

Then our wants seemed to disappear when he withdrew into full-blown drug addiction.

Around the time of his first stay in the Priory, something wonderful happened. My niece Leela was born.

I have never been broody, but I had never felt such a sharp tug in my belly as I did when I held her. She was like a little old man, scrunched up, with big eyes, so much potential and hope packed into her tiny little body, radiating from her in waves, and I fell in love with her the minute I saw her. I knew then that I wanted to try for children, but I also knew that Rob needed to be in recovery for a decent length of time before this could happen.

We continued our wonderful, sedate life for a few months. Christmas came and went and it was the best one we had as a family. Leela was gurgling in her stroller, Daisy was lolloping around, Rob cooked the most spectacular leg of lamb.

Nearly five months in, he looked as though he was going to make it to his six-months-clean mark – which is when I said we'd try for a baby.

While shopping one day in Boots, he pointed at some prenatal vitamins. 'Are you sure we aren't getting ahead of ourselves?' I asked.

'Ah, go on, we're nearly there. Also, they're the gummy bear kind so they taste good too.'

I picked them off the shelf reluctantly; it was hard to shake the worry. My body drew itself into a tight line and avoided sex; it already knew what my mind didn't want to accept – that we were nowhere near ready. That our newfound stability was still only a shell, barely strong enough to contain the both of us.

The background to all of this was that Rob had lost one of his contracts and was finding it hard to secure more work.

I was also aware that he hadn't been applying for jobs. By now I understood that, although my husband appeared confident, the prospect of rejection had been crippling him in the last few years. I knew the loss of the contract had knocked his confidence, and, if we weren't careful, it could knock his recovery off course too.

A week later, we moved again, to nearby St Margaret's – the Hampton house we'd been renting had endemic damp, and our landlord was being an arsehole about it. But I couldn't shake the feeling that something was going wrong with Rob.

His eyes seemed dead again – he said from the exhaustion of moving things around. Then he caught a cold and assured me it was definitely a virus. He asked to borrow some money while he waited for some jobs to come through.

When I asked him if he was all right, he said he'd just found the change of environment a bit stressful. 'But it's all okay,' he reassured me. 'You're being a bit paranoid, honey.'

It wasn't until we went to Martin's that I knew something was very, very wrong.

Martin has a wonderful, restful house in the south of France. I met him through Mal, and Mal met him through work; they're both in finance. At least once a year, Mal and I visit him there and we talk trash and unwind from city life.

Martin is beautiful, Scottish and about fifteen years older than us. He was sensible with his money and invested some of it in this magnificent stone house with green shutters. If I close my eyes and think of Martin's, I can see a bright blue sky, fields of sunflowers stretching towards it, the orange canvas of his poolside umbrellas, a pale pink, cold, glass of wine, and a sense of peace and relaxation I simply don't get anywhere else.

Summer is our favourite time to go there. We lie by the pool until we turn into dark chestnuts; the wine sends us to a place perfect for afternoon naps and Martin takes care of everything. His preference for taking charge is our gain – we don't cook, we just clean and help clear the tables after meals of beef Wellington, mozzarella and tomato salad, croissants and ham, slow-cooked lamb and slabs of cheese. There is Kylie, *Glee* and Michael Jackson on rotation, as we are all lazy and forget to bring CDs, and in the evening we flop on white sofas and watch the latest bad box set.

In winter, the fire comes on and, after long walks in the snow, we uncurl amid the crackle of logs, cosy blankets and glasses of red wine.

For Mal and me, Martin's place had always been a little haven, and it was a big deal that Rob had been invited.

But Rob ruined it. The weeks leading up to the trip had been fraught. I was feeling the strain of paying for everything and we'd been fighting over his inability to find new work.

The weekend break started promisingly, however. On the flight over there, Rob was on top form, asking Martin if he wanted to join the 'Silverback Club' which was 'for men whose ball hair was starting to go grey'.

'We Silverbacks have to stick together, Martin,' he said sagely.

But the morning after we arrived at the house, it became

clear that everything was not all right. He made Martin buy calamari and prawns with the grand promise that he was going to cook them. They sat untouched and rotting in the fridge.

He spent almost the entire visit in bed, sweating and tired, and by the time we got back to London, I was sick to my stomach. I was fed up; I felt trapped, tired and pissed off that my weekend had been spent worrying about Rob, whether he was okay, that he had spent no time with my friends, that I had to field questions about whether he was all right. Because something was going on and he *still* wasn't telling me what it was.

All in all, a bad trip. When I came back, haggard and unrested, the first thing a work colleague said was: 'Jesus Christ. You look like you've had whisky for breakfast.'

A couple of weeks later, I had to fly to a big summit in Munich, and was concerned when he didn't answer any of my calls or text to see if I had arrived safely.

'Rob – is everything all right? What is going on over there?' I messaged. No reply.

My boss and I went out for bratwurst and pale beer under a grey wintery sky, while my insides furrowed with worry. I eventually got a text from him saying everything was good at home but he was feeling a bit fluey.

When I got home he was very chipper. 'Baby,' he said, bouncing around after he had shown me his NA chip for being six months clean, 'I've got something to ask you.

'I've been in a work rut and I think it would do me a lot of good to go to Sheffield to visit S. Go for a few walks and so on. I'll take Daisy with me – you won't have to worry about a thing, I promise.'

I went very quiet. This was starting to feel worryingly familiar. The exhaustion. The flu. The borrowing of money again. The 'trip' away, which in previous times had actually been withdrawal.

'Rob,' I said, trying to hide how upset I was, the dread filling my insides like cement, 'have you relapsed?'

'What? No! Of course not, honey. My recovery means everything to me, and I wouldn't do that to you, I promise. I just feel like London has been crowding me in a bit, and I think it might do some good to get some space.'

'It's just that before when you went away, you know . . . '

'I know. And I'm so sorry for that. But honestly, I would say if something was wrong. I'll call every day, and I promise I'll be back in action when I come back. Clean husband, right? Babies, hmm?' he said and nuzzled my hair.

So he went, and I visited my sister in Brighton while he was away.

As we sat around the table for dinner, my brother-in-law Shabby asked me a few questions. He had most recently seen Rob a couple of weeks ago, when he had taken our dishwasher over to them as we didn't need it in our new flat.

Shabby is an exceptional cook, and I just wanted to concentrate on the incredible meal he'd prepared, of fried courgettes, orzo and pesto and chicken stuffed with goat's cheese and spinach. No such luck.

*How was he? Was he sleeping well? Had I noticed anything out of the ordinary? Why did he seem so out of it when he came over to drop the dishwasher off?*

I grew irritated, thinking, *Why the fuck is he interrogating me, I just want to eat!*

He apologised when he saw how angry I had become, but said: 'Poo, I'm really sorry but I'd be remiss in not asking you. Everything you've told me points to relapse.'

I put my head in my hands, and the full misery of the last few weeks, what I'd tried so hard to avoid, pressed down on me. On the one hand, I hoped against hope that he hadn't relapsed. On the other, I knew that if he had, it would allow me permission to ask for a separation, to see through the ultimatum I had given him six months before. 'I don't know how much longer I can do this for. How much longer I can bear this. At least if he has relapsed I know what's going on, and I wouldn't be a monster for wanting to leave,' I whispered, hating myself for it.

I didn't know what to do. How on earth would I find the strength to break up with the love of my life, if I had to?

They both hugged me at the dinner table. Later that evening, I called Rob. I kept asking him the same question over and over: 'Have you relapsed? Just tell me the truth.' He denied it, over and over.

Then finally, late at night, a text. 'You're right. You're

always right. When you think I've relapsed I have. I'm so sorry. I was in such a bad place. I'm so scared of losing you.'

This time, it was different. It wasn't just that I'd been lied to again, made to feel paranoid, that he'd undermined all the trust in our marriage. It wasn't even that he'd fooled the people at NA – the one group he was supposed to feel he could be honest with – to get his six-month chip.

It was the babies.

However noble the reasons, I couldn't be with someone who would bring children into such chaos. And now that I had some notion of what it was like to feel protective over a child, in the way that I felt about Leela, it made me angry to think about these children who would have been conceived in a lie.

'Poo,' my sister said gently, 'he sent me a text two days ago asking me if I thought it would be a good idea to have a vow renewal ceremony to celebrate him being clean.'

I read the text in horror. During his recovery, I spoke about how I wanted to renew our vows if we managed to get him sober, because I felt cheated of my wedding day.

The text revealed that Rob wasn't just lying to me, he was lying to himself, and that, even with the threat of losing everything hanging over him, he would continue to lie. This was that 'fixity' Prof. Williams spoke about. How could he ever get real, proper help when he couldn't fully acknowledge or accept his problems? When he believed, against all the evidence, that he could outsmart something that had beaten him over and over again? How could he even hope to break the cycle of destruction that had taken almost everything away from him?

And although I was in love with him, although I could never imagine loving anyone else as much as I loved him and would always love him, whatever our future together, I had reached the end of the road where I could help him – and, most importantly, where I wanted to help him.

Our marriage was over.

*Desperation, when met with the possibility of hope, pushes people to do incredible things. Move cars with their bare hands, swim miles to get to shore, survive for days underneath earthquake rubble without food or water.*

*I've learned there's a desperation that follows grief in a way like no other. So desperate are you, so hopeful for a snatch of the person you have lost, there are endless tricks your mind will play on you.*

*We wonder where they are. We wonder if they are the clouds smeared against the sky, the edge of birdsong filling the trees, in the radio waves that make a song they loved burst into sound.*

*On the day we buried Rob, when our eyes couldn't quite believe he was lying still and silent on sheepskin, we said the rain was him causing mischief, the sun was him giving us lightness when we felt so dark.*

*In the back and forth of rain and sun, double rainbows lit the sky, arcs of fire sweeping across the broad Auckland blue. Back in England, a different continent, a different hemisphere and season, rainbows soared as well, the sky tracing a fingertip from its mouth to the earth.*

*In so many cultures and religions, a rainbow is the sign of the earth and sky connecting, otherworldliness meeting humanity.*

*In Greek mythology, it is the goddess Iris delivering messages between the gods and mortals.*

*In Maori culture, it is the god Uenuku, who fell in love with the mist-maiden Hinewai – a beautiful woman who would disappear in the morning dawn and who asked him to keep their relationship a secret but he broke his promise.*

*In Hinduism, it can represent several things. One is that it is the bow of Indra, the mighty god of thunder and war, and from it he shoots arrows formed from lightning. But the one I love the most is the 'rainbow body' that comes from Buddhism and Hinduism – a person who has died but achieved ultimate oneness and peace, and resides in the motes of colour straddling the atmosphere.*

*Rainbows may seem to come from the realm of unicorns and sparkles, but there is a metaphor more poignant, more truthful than any of those things.*

*A rainbow only ever appears after the rain, after the clouds have gathered. It is only ever called into being when darkness arrives and then departs. It is hope that the storm will pass; it is wonder in its simplest form.*

*We wish we could look at it forever, but its beauty exists because of its transience.*

*On that day it wasn't physics. Indra laid down his bow, Uenuku had seen our pain and desperation. Iris stayed silent to allow Rob the chance to ease our misery. And for a brief moment, as we lifted our heads to the sky searching for the light in a storm of such sadness, he did.*

# Chapter Ten

It was Valentine's Day, 2015. I remember each step on the staircase of the train station. I took each one with both feet, like a child who was unable to stretch their legs any further.

I passed the newsagent's where Rob ordered his comic books, the greengrocer's that sold freesias, his favourite flowers, in big buckets. Further along, the baby shop.

Fuck me, the baby shop. Mustn't cry. Mustn't cry.

'I've put the breakfast bar chairs together,' Rob texted while I was on the train, as if everything was normal, as if he hadn't just told me he'd spent the best part of four weeks lying to me.

Rob had returned from Sheffield the night before, I was arriving from Brighton, strengthened by my sister's love.

But it wasn't enough. I knew when I arrived home, that was it. My life as I knew it was over. Our trips to the gym. Coffee at Gosia's. Fighting over Terry Pratchett books. Watching *Doctor Who*. Looking at the bluebell patch near my parents' house. Christmas dinners. Making the bed together. Saying *I love you.*

It was so much more than sadness and lost memories, it was the future dissolving at my feet.

*I can't do this.*

When I stepped through the door, Daisy launched herself at me, wagging her tail and whacking me with it. Oh my God, *Daisy.*

Rob popped his head round the corner, his face filled with concern. But he also looked terrible, like he hadn't slept in a thousand years. Heroin sick.

I looked at him. I placed the two of us and our dog, our unborn babies, all of the things we loved, in an imaginary snowglobe. I knew that once these words came out of my mouth, they would forever be preserved, but I could never touch or enter that world again. I let those seconds and minutes last as long as I could before I said: 'We need to talk.'

We sat in the lounge. Me on the blue sofa. Him on the floor, fussing with his hands, one of his thumbs a blunt little mallet from when his mother accidentally shut it in a door when he was a child.

*Thumbie, I love you*, I once said and kissed the tip.

The three-quarter-length nude Balinese bust we bought on our honeymoon oversaw the proceedings with her one broken nipple. So much of our life in one tiny room, each object a story, a connection, guy ropes rippling back and forth to one another, two hearts connected by a million different things.

'Rob, I love you,' I began. 'But we had a conversation last year where I told you that if you lied to me again, I would ask you for a separation.'

'Honey,' he began.

I held up my hand. 'Please. If I don't get the words out, I may never find the strength. I love you. So much. But I can't live like this any more. I hate my life. I am asking you for a separation.'

I remember how his face fell. He closed his eyes and kept them closed. He had expected it to be different, I could tell that much.

I don't remember the words, just the colours everything was painted in. So much red, our hearts bleeding for each other; my anger that he'd let me down, his anger that I couldn't forgive him. Covered in blue, the sadness that washed over us in waves; it drenched our lives in ice water trying to stamp out the spark. Everything black, save for one gleaming strand of gold, a tiny sliver of hope that Rob could somehow turn this around.

I asked for a three-month separation, and if in that time he could show me how he wanted sobriety and a better life for himself, not just for me, then I would consider taking him back. And in that time, there were no guarantees – I needed time to think, time I hadn't ever had while ping-ponging between Rob's recovery, hospital stay and constant worry that I'd return home to something horrific.

For so long, even during my heart surgery, our relationship

had been about Rob's ever-changing physical state and emotions – how he was feeling that day, his wants, his needs. I'm not saying he didn't want to put me first; I'm saying he was often incapable of it because of the fluctuating nature of his illness.

I needed space to breathe.

During our separation, he was going to go to New Zealand. Many people wondered why, and whether it was the right thing to do.

At that time, it was the only thing to do.

When Rob was strong in his recovery, several months before the events that brought us to that terrible point, there was a guy called William who lived in a bus stop near our house. Rob knew him from NA and asked if this guy could come and stay on our couch.

'I don't want to seem like the biggest asshole,' I said, 'but no. This is some random dude and I have my wedding jewellery in the house.'

Later that day we drove past the bus stop and I saw a man sitting in it who looked like a university professor, reading a book. Neat with glasses, white and in his forties. 'That's William,' Rob said. I looked closer and saw the sleeping bag next to him and a suitcase, containing presumably everything he owned.

William looked like your bank manager. The man who

would teach your kids. He looked like every commuter you brush against on your way to work in the morning.

'What happened?' I asked Rob in wonder. 'He looks so . . . normal.'

Rob shrugged. 'He was an addict. He lost his wife and kids, and then he lost his job.'

That simple. It was that easy to go from someone tethered to everything they loved, to someone on the streets.

I couldn't let that happen to Rob. I couldn't have him dying slowly in a bedsit. Freezing to death in an alleyway because he had nowhere to live. And there was a danger of it happening because I knew how hard he found it to ask for help, how his pride would kick in.

I didn't trust anyone else, only his family. He had, as he said, alienated many of his friends. It was a lot to ask, in any case – they had their own lives.

In matters like this, family was needed. And they happened to be in New Zealand. I knew Rob was scared about going back, and in hindsight this was probably tied to the demons he thought he'd left behind by dint of geography, yet had always been with him.

'The decision is yours, Bobbie,' I said, 'but it's the one that makes most sense. You'll have a time out, you won't have to worry about work and it'll be good to be somewhere that isn't London.'

He didn't want to be that far away from me or Daisy, but eventually he came to see it as a way of forging a new relationship with his parents and spending time with his family. We managed to find someone who was willing to foster Daisy through the Wood Green animal charity, so we knew she'd be looked after properly while he was away.

I was relieved because I knew that Rob would be safe, for a time. That he wouldn't fall down a crack and disappear.

Whenever I see a homeless person on the street, whatever state they are in – elegant like William or shaking in the withdrawal of some drug – I try to give them money. It's for three reasons. One is to say, *I see you. You are a human being, not trash on the street, and I see you.*

The second is because it can go on food or it might go on drugs. But I have to hope it will go on food and give them another day.

But the third, and most overwhelming, is that for all our family, for all of our friends, that person caught in a battle raging far beyond the street upon which they sit, that could have been Rob.

We had seven weeks until he was due to leave for New Zealand and, in that time, we were going to stay together under the same roof. On the first day, we didn't know what to do about sleeping in the same bed.

'I'll respect whatever you want,' Rob said. He looked so defeated.

'We're sleeping in the same bed,' I said firmly.

At first, I couldn't comprehend that I wouldn't be able to kiss him. I tried to kiss him and he pulled away. It's hard to explain without making him sound noble because there was a lot in that seven weeks which was hard and horrible thanks to Rob – but I knew why he wouldn't kiss me. It wasn't because he didn't want to. It's because, in that regard, he was a better person than me and knew I had made a tough choice, and kissing each other would only complicate things for me.

He wanted me to make the decision to stay with him with a clear head, not out of nostalgia or because of muddled feelings.

Certainly, there were also shades of martyrdom in him. We were on the path of separation and he would see it through on bloodied stumps if he had to. 'We made a promise to each other,' he said.

He saw some of this as penance, professing to go vegetarian as Christian saints and Hindu sadhus had done. 'Just eat the fucking chicken, Rob,' I said savagely. 'Salvation isn't going to come through chickpeas.'

Prue was going to fly over to give us support, and Rob was imminently about to go into the Priory for a second stint. The night before he was due to go in, he offered to cook dinner and I came home to find him with a hoarse, high-pitched voice.

I laughed and said: 'What happened? You sound like a lay-dee.'

'I think I'm coming down with something. Maybe tonsillitis,' he replied. I'd been the same when I once had tonsillitis, so I just nodded.

His voice continued to be hoarse for a few days.

When I saw Rob's admittance notes after he died, it said that he had tried to hang himself before coming in. My blood ran cold.

An evening of dinner and talking could instead have been coming home to find his body hanging from the bannister. And I had *laughed*. I had *laughed* at his voice and he had gone on with the charade.

His stay in the Priory this time was different. There was no swagger, no stories about the other patients. He was broken as a person and looked it. He had gone in there having taken heroin the day before, and so rather than engaging in groups, he spent the first few days in withdrawal.

When I visited him he was gaunt, like a skeleton. Where was the colour in his cheeks? The strong forearms I loved? I was looking at a shell; the man inside was crumbling.

We sat in an empty therapy room and he could barely look at Daisy. He started crying about children, our children that we would probably never have. Then that made me cry. 'I pictured what they would look like,' I said through my tears. But instead of holding me, it was a moment of such pain, such sharp regret and loss, that he asked if I minded leaving because he needed to be alone.

I think he realised that even if we managed to patch

things up, he wouldn't ever be well enough to raise kids. A child deserves safety, love and consistency. How, in good conscience, could he put another person, someone he loved, in the chaos of his own addiction? And the blow was even harder because right up to his last relapse, he believed it was completely possible. In a letter to my cousin Prarthana at the time, back when they were teaching each other Maori and Tulu – my family's language – he wrote: 'Today's Maori word: *Aroha*. Meaning love. Spoken like a wolf, and my daughter's name.'

When he came out of hospital, days were punctuated with chaos – I'd wake to find him gone, having left the house in the middle of the night to stay with NA friends. My mornings would start with panic, trying to figure out where he was until I received a text saying he was all right.

One of the hardest things was the disentanglement of our lives, the utter mundane mixed with the deeply personal. He needed to wrap up things like his gym membership before leaving, cancel work insurance, put his things in the loft.

In the midst of all of this, we argued like we had never argued before – I was so angry that he'd thrown our marriage away, that he'd thrown *me* away. I was sorry Prue was caught in the middle of it, but at the same time her presence was an immeasurable help, especially because I needed to talk to someone about what was really going on.

He'd say things like: 'You know, if you were a bartender, I can't help but wonder ...'

'Wonder what, Rob?' I replied, my jaw clenching at the subtext of what he was saying. That if I was a bartender, I'd be more focused on him and would have more time. Less career-minded. That maybe this mess was *my* fault because, y'know, I hadn't spent *quite* enough time worried sick and helping him.

If I was the type of career woman who worked long hours and weekends and cancelled plans with loved ones, I could completely understand it. But I'm a Type A, who works like a laser-focused motherfucker during the time I'm in the office. I leave on time, I sleep like a boss and I always, *always* prioritise my family over work. This is because I know that, when I eventually die, I'm never, ever going to say I wish I'd spent more time in the office.

'Because,' I continued, not allowing him to reply, 'if I was a bartender, you wouldn't have had private treatment. Or access to the best doctors. You would've been left to rot and die in this shitty, poor excuse for a mental health service that we have in this country. So put that in your fucking pipe and smoke it.'

It would've been more dramatic had he not actually been smoking a cigarette at the time.

But who was this person? My husband – my real husband – was proud of me, and of my job. When we started dating he was glad he was with someone who could pay their own way. This was the illness manipulating his mouth like a marionette – trying to rationalise and bargain the wrong things. Avoiding insight at all costs.

Despite wonderful nuggets like this, genuinely, deep down, there was a spark in me that hoped Rob could find his way. That he would hit rock bottom and come back up.

A week before he left, towards the end of March, spring had arrived.

It seemed wrong that amid all of this anger and sadness, cherry blossom appeared in pink hopeful puffs, daffodils shook their yellow heads at us from the ground, and tulips, brief but bright, puckered their lips as we moved about our lives in grey.

We went for one last dinner at our favourite Italian restaurant, having almost argued our way out of the evening. We wanted one night when we didn't fight, didn't cry and didn't get sad.

'We need to conduct the rest of the week with dignity and love,' he texted. I agreed.

At dinner, I ordered crab linguine dusted with cheese; Rob had tiger prawns and clams. We looked at each other and felt that connection back to a place of pure love. Whatever the reality, whatever happened between us, we knew that our bond existed in that place.

Somehow we had an evening where we felt loved, we discussed the true state of our relationship, the possibility of not being able to reconcile, and walked home.

There was a moment I remember perfectly. We held hands and walked down a lamp-lit path that ran through a small park, connecting a canal to the road our house sat on. I could hear the water rushing past in the stream. See the fringe of cherry blossom up ahead, the earth stirring itself into a lush green, and a clear sky of stars looking down.

We stopped along the path and Rob cried because he started talking about babies. We held each other and hugged underneath the moonlight, and something told me in that instant that this was the last time we would ever stand in that spot together.

I tried to remember every detail: the way he smelled, how his arms felt around me, the blossom under a night sky. I felt his sobs pass through me.

Then when we got home, as we were fishing around for the door key, I asked him what would happen to all of his plant pots crammed into the tiny front garden, little green stubs waiting for the right season. And he said: 'Well, they'll start to do something wonderful soon.'

And then I started crying. For the flowers that would arrive in the absence of my husband, for the irrepressible nature of life, that things go on living even when you feel like everything in your world is dying.

A week later, Rob relapsed on alcohol, turning up at 3am drunk and unable to stand.

The following morning he was remorseful but said, 'It's not a relapse' and, 'It's not a big deal.' But I knew how big a deal it was. By this point I was angry, but I wasn't surprised. And the anger felt different this time – it felt like I wasn't carrying our future in my hands. Our season was over, and it would take a miracle for us to find our way back.

After my anger exhausted itself, we spent the day together. We shared the same bed and our limbs were wrapped around each other for the last time. There was no sex, just us under the sheets with our pyjamas on, being as close as you could possibly be.

The next morning, he walked me to my car. I was driving to my parents' to spend some time with my family and I couldn't be at home when Prue and he left for the airport, it would be too hard.

I remember the exact spot on the street. The sun was shining, the leaves on the hedge glossy, young and light green.

'You are the love of my life, Rob,' I said, holding his face in my hands. 'I'm going to miss you so much. Please, please look after yourself.'

'I love you,' he replied. 'I will always love you. You will always be perfect and beautiful to me.'

And then he kissed me. Properly kissed me. From the earth's core, past rock and roots and up through our toes, it came from that place where big love lives.

It was lightning and fire, and it was the last time we would ever kiss.


I felt how keenly he reached out to me when he was in Auckland. I felt his heartache and yearning across the ocean, wiggling past sea urchins and clownfish, over the backs of sharks and through the blowholes of whales.

We were in contact every day at first, and then kept in touch via email, Skype and talking on the phone. The disapproval from the people in my life was not just palpable, it was vocalised pretty loudly. We shouldn't be in contact as much, they said. 'Yes, yes,' I said to their faces, and behind closed doors I ignored them.

None of them understood the complexities of your loved one having depression, and who was to lay out the terms of separation but the two of us?

'It's not fair, Poorna,' they said. 'If you know things are over, you need to put him out of his misery.'

But I didn't know things were over. Or if I did, I wasn't ready to articulate it. I didn't know what I wanted, and I was going through the first bout of depression I had ever experienced, caused by the breakdown of my marriage.

We didn't break up because I stopped loving him. We broke up because I loved myself enough to realise that I deserved to be in a relationship where I wasn't lied to, and because the longer I stayed with him, the less I respected myself, and eventually I would stop loving him.

The idea that I wouldn't ever want the best for Rob, that a day would come when I wouldn't care what happened to him, was simply unthinkable – I couldn't stand that.

So when we separated, I was in love with him.

These people expected me to be clear-headed and to make

huge decisions around things I barely felt capable of acknowledging. In fact, it was so overwhelming I needed to sign off work for two weeks.

When we Skyped, I wanted to be with him. I saw the books behind him at Prue's house and when I closed my eyes I was there with a cup of tea and a biscuit. I saw him on the deck at Felicity's and I could smell the roses in her front garden.

But, at the same time, I had a creeping suspicion that something was wrong in New Zealand, and I was worried that he might have started drinking again. There was a slightly bizarre edge to some of his messages.

As usual, any misgivings I had were muddled by signs of recovery. He signed up to a detox programme that seemed like it would help him turn things around.

'But that would mean I'm here longer than the three months,' he said, squinting at me through the screen. Three months was the period of separation I'd asked for, and said we'd have a chat about what to do with our relationship after that.

'Rob, whatever happens with us, your recovery is more important than our relationship. I've already told you that,' I replied.

The problem, it seemed to everyone else, was that Rob was placing so much hope in us being able to reconcile, while in my mind, that was going to be very unlikely. 'But he knows this,' I told them. 'We've spoken about it.' Under no circumstances had I tried to fool him or lead him on. I had been very clear that the future did not look good for us.

This manic hope was pure Rob – it was the inability to accept the circumstances while at the same time being aware of the reality.

I suggested that we take a break from talking about our relationship for a while, but he couldn't help himself. He sent me an email.

I don't ask that you respond in any way. I just need to get it out.

So where we're at is either a beginning or an ending. I believe there's a parallel with recovery, in that our marriage is at the kind of rock bottom that brings people into recovery. We either go our separate ways or we bring our marriage into recovery and use this rock bottom to build something much stronger, durable, rewarding and powerful.

I believe we have a true love, one I personally would have no hope of replicating in the rest of a life without you in it. I believe our marriage is worth us fighting for.

And I also understand very, very clearly why that is something you're asking yourself whether you can do, whether you can take the risk, whether you would be made to feel a fool.

Despite him saying he didn't want an answer, he did. Despite me saying I didn't want to talk about it, he did.

Those words were a bolt of clarity that cut through my mental fog: I didn't have it in me to trust him. I didn't have the energy to rebuild our life because I knew – however hard he tried – that it would fall to me to do so.

And so, eventually, eighteen days later, when I finally mustered the courage, I wrote him a letter saying I didn't see a beginning, only an ending. I told him I loved him, that he was the only man I had ever loved like that, but that too much had happened for me to think things would be different.

He called me. He soothed me as I cried down the phone. 'I'm sorry, I'm so sorry Rob, I love you but I can't.'

'Hey, hey, honey,' he said, 'it's okay. I understand. I love you, okay?' In that conversation, his voice was calm, full of love and compassion. He said everything I needed to hear, perhaps things I didn't deserve to hear. He said he wanted happiness and peace for me, he said he would be all right. That he was going to try to fix his life and find value in it.

But over the next seven days, he went up and down dramatically. The next day he could barely talk. Then he asked me not to contact him while sending me texts asking why I hadn't replied. He said, 'We should speak one last time' and I would go, 'What the hell do you mean, one last time?' This went on and on. I couldn't win.

He was at Felicity's, in her back garden, when we had our

last Skype chat. I was in my bedroom, wrapped up in blankets at eleven in the morning, still signed off work.

'I don't know how I'm ever going to be happy again,' he said and started crying. 'There will never be anyone but you.'

I looked at this man, my husband, and wondered how we had gotten here. I wanted to hold him, see him, touch him. The thought of us never being husband and wife again seemed wrong, considering how much we loved each other.

We started talking slowly, then we made a joke about someone we knew and started laughing. He smiled at me and said: 'I love you. I will always love you.'

*I love you too.* I think the words. I think them with all my heart. But I hear everyone else's voice in my head about leading him on and so I don't say it back.

We are in a fight.

It's the kind of fight that makes no sense, but I don't think I'm just fighting Rob. I think that bitch depression and that bastard addiction have wrapped their tentacles around him again and are doing the talking.

His messages are short, abrupt. They sound like they have been written by a robot. They make no sense, they are rude, they are not written in the language of our relationship at all.

One of the messages that was not rude informs me that I will soon be receiving a handwritten letter. A huge letter that details all the things he has already spoken about. Great awareness of how he has let me down, but grand promises of what he can and will do to get our marriage back.

I do not know this at the time, but he is pinning everything on this letter. He thinks this letter will be the thing that changes my mind, that will make me see the light and be won over by big love.

It is the hope of a teenager – that love will save the day and a letter can change the world.

But if I, a person who has broken up with the love of my life, who has done so despite being in love with him, fought like a she-bear for this marriage, if *I* have given up, the reasons for me doing so must be colossal. It is going to take more than a letter.

I no longer live in a world where love can save the day. I have learned the most painful lesson of all: that a person cannot save you from your sadness, and you cannot save them from theirs.

I wake to messages from Rob, asking me if I've received the letter. I say yes, and that it was a beautiful letter, but it won't change my mind.

He sends me a message saying that he can't do this any more. It's an odd message, and I ask him where he is. I call him, he doesn't answer.

'ROB ARE YOU SAFE?' I text.

I am so mad. He just drops a message like that and then doesn't answer. So I yell at him, I tell him how mad I am, that I don't want to speak to him if he's going to be like this, that I'm sick of worrying.

He doesn't answer.

I go for a run, the anger steaming off me in the morning air. I am getting angrier and angrier by the second. I come back, and text him again. This time he replies that he can't do it. He says he's an addict, bankrupt, mentally ill, has lost his family, will never see his niece grow up, it is too much.

It finally dawns on me what he is doing. I beg. I tell him I love him. I ask him to pick up the phone.

He tells me it is not my fault, but I don't get to talk to him on the phone because I ended our marriage in a letter. 'Please let me say goodbye to my parents in peace.' It's him but it doesn't sound like him.

'Rob, please, honey, please,' I plead. 'You promised me.'

After he told me about the suicide attempt with the car eighteen months before, I made him promise. I sat him down, held his hands, looked him in the eye and made him swear he would never, ever do that again.

'I'm sorry,' he replies by text, 'but I made that promise for us. There is no us.'

I know where he is trying to get to, and I am clawing at him but his body is turning to sand and an ill wind is blowing him through the cracks of a door, to a place I can't get to. I can't hold on, I can't hold on, he is slipping through my fingers.

His last message to me is: 'Look I'm sorry.' But I don't actually believe it. Not that he isn't sorry, but that he is going to go through with it.

During the course of the day, there is a panic, an itch beneath my skin. I get worried phone calls from Prue, Wesley, Monique.

But I'm sure, I'm so sure he's going to turn up sheepish and hungover. We are all glued to our phones; we are all watching the time-stamp on WhatsApp.

*Last seen today 10.30am.*

A full twelve hours later, we still haven't heard from him. The time-stamp hasn't changed. It's now morning in New Zealand, night-time in England. The police have been called, they are looking for him. A helicopter is combing the area they traced his last mobile phone signal to.

I do something I haven't done for three years. I get on my knees and I pray in front of the gods. I offer them everything. I offer my soul. I offer my heart. I offer my life for his.

At 1am, I get a phone call. It's Prue and she's crying. 'They've found him,' she says. 'They've found him. He's dead, Poorna. I'm sorry, I'm so sorry.'

My breath grows shallow, my throat constricts. I feel thunder crack across the world.

'Are you sure it isn't a mistake? Someone else?' I ask because anything, anything but this.

'No,' she replies in the softest whisper.

'Oh my God. Oh my God,' I cry.

But there is no God. I might as well be saying the word cheese.

People will say afterwards, 'He's with God now,' 'God take care of you, my child.' I know exactly where God was not on that night – he was not by my husband's side. During his moments of recovery, Rob had gone to his temple for salvation, had visited his churches with his soul in his hands asking for help and was unheard. He had forsaken Rob.

God can sit and swivel.

I tell Prue I'm coming on the next flight. I tell her I love her. I tell David I love him. I tell them to hold on. Then it hits.

I run to my parents' room and I'm wailing; it's primal, so jagged with pain that comes from the deepest grief that my soulmate, my love, my best friend is gone forever.

My sister is downstairs, visiting for the weekend with Leela, then still quite tiny and asleep. She hears the noise and comes upstairs. They all hold me, wrap their arms in a tangle like I'm a small rubber band about to fall away.

Priya takes me downstairs and sits with me on the sofa, our knees pulled up to our chest. It's like we're kids again but this time we're not covertly watching *A Nightmare on Elm Street* or Stephen King's *It*, this a real-life fucking horror show.

What tethers a person to their life?

Is it family? Love? All the books they ever read? A sense of worth? It can be all and some of those things, but the one thing that keeps us all here is the presence of hope. That as bad as things are, they will get better at some point. It is also the one thing that is absent in those who have taken their own lives.

Although there is no way of knowing a person's thought process in those final moments, a lot of men reach the point of no return because they aren't taught about emotional intelligence. Mr B said that they aren't encouraged to have social and psychological insight because it is seen as weakness.

But you can't save someone from themselves. And Rob could have had all the therapy, all the pills in the world, but unless he was able to unravel what his values were and why he had them, why he resorted to destroying himself when he felt he wasn't living up to the manly man ideal, he had no hope of ever finding a new path for himself.

Maybe Rob found it hard to seek help in a society that had muddled views about what depression is. But the key to making sense of why he sought oblivion was understanding how he saw himself in the world.

Mr B explained the thinking of Ken Wilber – the American writer who created the 'Integral Theory', a grid aimed at synthesising all human knowledge and experience as a way to explain how the individual is shaped as a person and how they see themselves in the world. Although I found Wilber's writing hard to digest, Mr B explained that a person is made up of the internal and external world.

'[Wilber] talks about the "I", the "We", the "It" and the "Its".

'The internal world is what's going on inside you and we know 80 per cent of how we act generally is subconscious. So, the way we interact, we're really only aware of 20 per cent of it. It is very important that we understand the "I" – what am I, how do I improve myself, how do I get more insight into myself internally? The "I" is when you were born, your colour, class and religion. Then there's the "We" – people we interact with, either closely or not so closely, lovers, friends, family and so on.

'Next, there's the external world. The "It" – so, what school you go to, the place you work. And the "Its" – the cultural context within which all this happens: so, "Rob was a white, middle-class male born in New Zealand to a Catholic family." Just giving people that information, they think they have a pretty good idea as to what that means. But really, do they?

'I interact with people from similar backgrounds – class, colour, creed, religion – but I do all that within the context of a predominantly white society. So the social and cultural context for me is: I will be well educated, therefore I will be successful; I'll have a family; I'll be an upstanding citizen, and what's expected of me is to be economically productive. So, if you are changing and challenging things, you have to look at *all* of these things. Most of our policies exist for the external world.

'We're going to improve public transport, we'll make the

health service better. Why are we going to do that? Well, transport gets people around, so they can get to work on time, so it's about the money, the GDP. Why should we have a health service? So people get well, and they can get back to being economically productive.

'We are stuck at a stage of human evolution where we are not dealing with emotional, social and psychological aspects of our lives.

'And the consequences are people who are not able to see that and who therefore use addictions to escape; then they get diagnosed with depression, and then get pills to treat that.'

He says that rather than slinging people on medication or writing them out of the workforce, we need a culture and workplace that respects mental health, that values people who are struggling and tries to work around them rather than rendering them invisible.

Hope is the most powerful force to be reckoned with. And I have to hope that day will come.


At some point I go to bed, but I just lie there rigid until the sun comes up. I think about Rob, and the immense sadness that he died in the woods. My brain can't help itself. It summons the texture of the rope in his hands, the despair he felt, the crunch of leaves under his feet, the mist of the wintery night air, and then him finally completing the act.

For hours, I can't move past the fact that he died alone,

thinking those awful things about himself. For hours, I wish I could have held his hand and kissed his forehead in that last moment. Told him how magnificent he was, how loved and kind and beautiful. I wonder how he felt, at the end. I can't bear to think of him crying.

Prue said he seemed calm and happy before he left the house. I wonder if death finally brought him peace.

And then I come back to reality, and I look about my bed. I find that I am in so many different pieces; I don't know how I will gather myself to get up and face the days to come.

It is hard thinking about Rob and peace, when I know – even then, even as I see the first sparks of the explosion ripping through our lives, setting the world on fire – that peace will be denied to us for many, many years.

*We are travelling across Lake Te Anau, a group of strangers united by a need to walk in the mountain air. The wind is whipping my hair into long streams; it feels like a river flowing back into the lake.*

*In the distance, I see the mountain range, and my heart lifts. It gently presses against a memory – the last time I was in a landscape like this was in the Himalayas, seven years ago.*

*Fiordland is a place that tumbles from one valley to another, waterfalls ribboning through the rock, deep, cold lakes gathered in extinguished craters, snowy peaks standing watch.*

*When I see the mountains layered against each other, solid yet so half-formed in the mist at their peaks, they look as if at any moment they may shift and move to reveal a gateway to a different world. I long for such a moment of escape.*

*How have seven years passed, when clambering over rocks and drinking hot tea in steel tumblers felt like yesterday?*

*Because I don't know anyone else on the boat, I stick to the outside and peer my head around the corner of plastic sheeting.*

*The wind has picked up and little waves are scudding across the surface of the lake.*

*Our boat is powerful, creating bigger waves at the front as it pushes through, and in the light they look like curls of fire and*

*ice, lit by the sun and quickly dissolving into the dark blue water.*
*It is mesmerising.*

*I look at the heart of it. I feel the cold spray of lake water on*
*my face. We are moving deeper and deeper into the centre of*
*nowhere, remote and beautiful.*

*For the first time in nine months, I am peaceful, I think.*

*And then, and then, I can't explain it, but in the midst of the*
*air, water and light, I feel Rob, and I feel something say:* I am
here. *And I am filled with him and I say: 'I love you, honey, I*
*miss you so much.'*

*And he says:* I love you too, and I'm so sorry. *The words just*
*arrive inside me; I don't know where they are coming from. I feel*
*him standing behind me, looking over at the water, but I know*
*what happened to Orpheus and so I'm not going to look back.*

*He's here! I want this moment to be perfect, but instead I*
*plead. I smell of desperation. 'Why did you leave me?'*

*I feel the anger in my voice, the vastness of my own loneliness.*

*Why am I wasting this unbelievable moment on negativity?*
*(Because it's how you feel, you tell yourself later.)*

*And he answers:* I wasn't leaving you, I was leaving myself.

# Chapter Eleven

I remember the exact moment I lost my faith.

It was 10 September 2012 at around eleven in the morning. I was lying on a stretcher in the operating room waiting for my heart operation, under lights so bright they pierced me clean.

I sensed the hurried movement of people going about their jobs, flicking switches, checking screens, and all of a sudden it left, like a breath, a gasp, a presence, so very much there and then so very much gone.

If I still had my faith, I would insist that, when I died, I be prepared according to Hindu rites: my body washed in milk, honey, yogurt and butter, turmeric placed on my face, and ideally set on a traditional wood pyre if the country I die in allows it.

However, now that I don't, my arrangements are a little bit more tbc.

All of the rites, from washing the body to holding a wake, share similarities with other cultures and belief systems, from Vikings to Islam. I believe this reveals something huge, vast, bigger than religion, and more about humanity and the rituals that help us all to digest grief regardless of what we worship.

Where Hinduism differs is that it hinges on *samsara*, or rebirth, and so death is softened by the hope and prospect of re-entering life once more.

Till death do us part, they say in the West, but even our wedding ceremony embodies the idea that death isn't the end for the two souls joining together. When Rob and I married, we walked round the fire seven times, to bind us together for seven lifetimes, a union seared in flame.

'But Bobbie, how do we know which lifetime we're at?' I asked a few days later on our honeymoon, when we were spreadeagled, fat and brown, on sun loungers.

'Like, what if we're at lifetime number six and we only have one left to go?'

He smiled and pressed my hand.

Because we always cremate our dead, and because the only people I knew who had died were my grandparents, I had no idea what was actually involved when you're the person at ground zero. The logistics, the surreal normality of things like paperwork in a situation that is so far removed from normal you don't know how you'll navigate the next hour, let alone the rest of your life.

Prue asked me if I wanted a cremation or a burial for Rob, and in between emails pinging back and forth on my way to New Zealand, I felt quite strongly it would be a burial.

When someone dies well before their time, far sooner than they should have done, there is a desperate, hungry need to keep them on earth a while longer. To have a place to talk, cry and laugh, to tell them your fears and dreams, even if these are just ghost conversations never quite able to take form.

Also, when your husband dies prematurely and you're Hindu – even an ex-Hindu – you tend to get a bit twitchy about cremation. After all, we once did *sati*. This is the practice of self-immolation, where widows would volunteer or be forced on the pyre of their dead husbands as a final tribute.

I mean, seriously – fuck that. Surely the final tribute is living; telling stories of your love, making sure his memory lives on.

'I think it's a completely missed opportunity,' said Mal with absolute seriousness, 'that airports don't have a shop that just sells digestive biscuits and Twinings tea. Business would be booming.'

We were in Heathrow, running on little sleep, on our way to New Zealand for the funeral.

Although her business idea was terrible, I needed scraps of normality like that to tether me to the world. Mal is very passionate about how very few countries outside of Britain actually do decent tea. And, at a time like this, I needed something as safe, comforting and insane as a diatribe on tea.

I didn't have a script for any of this. I knew from films how people reacted in times of grief. Some lay down and didn't get up. Some couldn't stop crying. Some packed a bag and left their lives entirely, without a word.

But that's not how I felt. The emotions were huge and they swung so wildly, so frequently between one another – hope, rage, anger, hopelessness, sadness, love, forgiveness, fear – that it was like stepping across vast ice floes scattered over a sunless sea. I felt like a stranger in my own mind, but I also knew I was capable of functioning on a basic level.

I didn't feel guilty when I laughed; in fact, I felt relief I was able to do so in between the moments that were so black, unending and sad. I held on to them as tightly as someone panning for gold along a dark riverbed.

And I knew what people thought: we were separated, so did that mean ...?

YES! I wanted to scream. Of course it means I'm grieving as if I've lost my spouse because, guess what, he was my fucking spouse! He was the love of my goddamn life and, just because I had decided seven days prior that I couldn't live with his addiction any longer, it didn't make him any less mine! He was MINE. The loss was MINE. The love was MINE. And I was going to do right by him, and say goodbye to him with dignity and honour, with my head held high because THAT was the woman he married, not some wreck who couldn't tie her own shoelaces.

Mal was there despite my protestations that I didn't want anyone to come with me to New Zealand for the funeral. My parents offered and I shouted them down. They looked at me with fear and love, so out of their depth that they didn't push me.

'It doesn't matter what she said,' I heard my sister arguing with them downstairs. 'She needs someone with her even if she doesn't know it. She needs family. If I have to strap Leela to me and breastfeed her on the plane so I can go, I'll do it.'

I was upstairs, pacing around on the landing, and wanted to say: 'First, I'm not incapacitated, I know my own mind. Rob's family *is* my family. I don't need you guys there. You're just going to get in the way.'

But I lost that battle and when Mal dropped everything – the business trip she was due to leave on the next day – I was so glad to have her with me. To drink wine with, to laugh at the awful, weighty Oscar-worthy films Singapore Airlines had on offer. I also needed a witness to all of it, so that when I came back to England, I wasn't alone in my grief; that I could talk to someone about it.

The few days before leaving for New Zealand held so many terrible realisations. One was that I didn't have anything to wear to my own husband's funeral. Priya and I drove to Bluewater shopping centre and we ran from shop to shop in desperation. We stopped after the third shop and realised what we were doing and why we were doing it. We held each other outside Zara and just cried.

'Oh God, Poo,' she said.

'People are going to think we're lesbians breaking up with each other.'

'I don't care,' she snuffled.

At the airport, I received a long email from Prue. I was so worried that my mother-in-law would be angry at me, and I didn't know where my place was. His parents knew that I had told Rob I didn't think we could work things out.

But Prue said very firmly that I was his wife. 'We know he loved you with all his heart and spirit and mind and body and he never stopped loving you,' she wrote in a letter to me.

Everything to do with him and the funeral arrangements was my choice. Although I didn't know what the right answers were to all of the questions, I knew I had to do what was best for us.

Did I want him to have an autopsy? Absolutely not. (My mind screamed that we were discussing autopsies.)

Did I want Rob to come home the night before the funeral so people could pay their respects? Although I was unsure, I said yes, because I wanted people to be able to say goodbye and he was our boy, our beloved.

Did I want a burial or a cremation? Burial, absolutely burial. My mind couldn't cope with the thought of him turning to ash.

I thought of Daisy, how much she was a part of Rob, and how she would ever survive without him. Prue handled the whole thing; the lady who was fostering her said she would be happy to adopt her, and was I all right with that? I knew I couldn't look after Daisy and it would be kinder to her to be looked after by someone who had nothing to do with her old life.

I answered these on autopilot while clutching a green juice from Leon, and then tried to wrap my head around the reality of the situation. But none of it would be really real until I saw Rob.

Two days later, Mal and I were in the funeral home with Prue, David and Rob's brother John.

Ryan, the polite funeral director, greeted me with hushed tones. He was practical yet considerate, never fawning, and answered our questions patiently. He must see the looks of grief and horror on people's faces every day. How did he keep up the appropriate level of concern and interest? I wondered if this is something they learned at funeral school.

We were there to discuss details such as the burial plot, order of the funeral service. We had a choice of two plots, and when we visited the first, I wondered – having never picked a plot before – what the criteria were. Was it like renting a flat, where you had to check for certain things like damp, the suitability of your neighbours, whether it was south-facing?

The neighbours in this instance had big, black, shiny headstones. They had photographs of the deceased, pillars, fountains. I swear one had a turret.

Then things became more surreal when it came to choosing the coffin.

'Was Robert an eco-friendly man?' enquired Ryan.

I remembered Rob bollocking me for being lazy with the recycling, to which I replied: 'But you, as an environmental expert, said the planet was screwed no matter how much recycling we did!'

He just pointed at the bin, sternly.

'Well, Ryan,' I replied, 'he was certainly an environmentally *aware* man.'

We chose a rimu coffin, a wood native only to New Zealand. I didn't know what rimu looked like in the wild, but this was different to all the others in appearance and texture. When I finally did see one in its natural habitat, it was so very Rob-like in its unusual appearance. It was a conifer but instead of stiff needles pointing towards the sky, it had what looked like fronds of seaweed swaying towards the ground.

I held the handle on the side and felt it curve under my palm.

'The handles need to be comfortable,' said David, and I thought of the loved ones he must have carried, and now we were discussing his son.

Two days later I felt that handle slide against my palm as

I carried Rob into the church with Felicity on the other side, to James Taylor and Carole King singing 'You Can Close Your Eyes'.

We also visited the funeral home so I could see Rob. The room was called 'Rangitoto', named after one of Auckland's dormant volcanoes. I knew he was in there before they told me.

The name reminded me of the Maurice Gee books Rob bought for me, including *Under the Mountain*, which was set in Auckland. In it, the world is going to be consumed by subterranean alien monsters, and to get rid of them, two heroes, a boy and a girl, must throw special stones into the mouth of Rangitoto and Mount Eden. It was very Rob – aliens, apocalypse, and he was pretty proud old Maurice was a Kiwi.

When throwing the stone, the boy Theo has to recite: 'We bring you the gift of oblivion.'

Oblivion is such a very specific word used in the context of death by suicide. The person who has killed him or herself isn't doing so to get to paradise or to a better place – what they seek is a cessation of the self.

Mal held my hand. 'Do you want me to go in with you?'

I shook my head. Till death do us part, and I closed the door behind me.

Afterwards, she told me that she would never forget the sound of my cry when I saw Rob lying there. It began in my belly and shot up to the sky like a flare. It was him and it wasn't him. He was asleep, I told myself, but I saw the edges of blue blossoming around his mouth.

'How could you?' I cried. 'How could you? Why wasn't our love enough for you? How could you do this if you loved me? If you loved all of us?' And then it distilled into, 'My God, Rob, I wish we could have saved you. My love, my darling, my friend, the pain you must have been in, that this is where things ended.'

Who cut him down? Who washed his body? Did he have his wedding ring on? Did anyone cry when they found him? Who found him? Where did he die? What exact time did his light go out in the world?

I should have known. I should have been there.

The grief after a suicide is built on a thousand wishes, a million regrets. Divining the course of every word and gesture, every cancelled appointment and the phone call you didn't take. The last *I love you* that stayed in my mouth.

I looked at his face and I bartered everything to see the breath fill his cheeks and colour return to his skin. *Anything, anything, please, anything but this.* In that room, I believed his life could have been so easily saved and I had let him down.

In the months that followed, I knew better, but it still didn't ease the guilt and regret.


I needed to know why. I desperately needed to know why. I found myself in a world where loved ones were strangers, where I didn't know how to explain to people what had happened, where I was engulfed in the enormity of it all.

When I came back to London, it was very apparent that a death by suicide was viewed as shameful; that even talking about it was not acceptable.

A colleague said: 'You don't have to tell them what happened.' I think they thought they were being supportive but it gagged my grief; it made me feel like it was something I shouldn't reveal to people.

Not only did I have to deal with the grief that now flooded my life, but I discovered that the means of Rob's death made the legitimacy of my grief questionable, exposed his life to judgement from an invisible court, and that was if I even felt confident enough to talk about it.

In his book *Notes on Suicide*, Simon Critchley wrote:

Suicide, then, finds us both strangely reticent and unusually loquacious: lost for words and full of them. What we are facing here is an inhibition, a massive social, psychical and existential blockage that hems us in and stops us thinking.

We are either desperately curious about the nasty, intimate, dirty details of the last seconds of a suicide and seek out salacious stories whenever we can. Or we can't look at all because the prospect is too frightening.

On my side, there was rage, but not towards Rob.

Thinking back to that statistic – the biggest cause of death in men under forty-five – and considering the most recent one from the Ministry of Justice – that suicides among women in Britain have risen – it dawned on me how big this is and how deep this wall of silence goes.

The worst thing ever to happen to me was now something I couldn't talk about? I had to navigate other people's awkwardness and sanitise my grief?

I felt sick to my stomach at what happened to Rob.

So I wrote a blog, an open letter to Rob, telling the world what had happened to me, or rather telling the people in my world what happened to me. The colleagues who thought 'someone close to me had died' but were too polite to ask further; the friends who didn't know how I was feeling; my parents who needed to know that, regardless of how he died, I was going to honour him.

It went crazy – I mean, it was read by hundreds of thousands of people. I couldn't believe it. I got many emails privately that kept me going through some of my darkest days – letters from people who said it saved them to know someone else knew how they felt, those who reached out in compassion and had good advice because they had already walked the same path as me, and those who were on the same path as Rob.

One letter that resonated with me strongly was one in which the author described their own journey towards and away from suicide.

I had few emotions left besides despair. That's the part
that many people don't understand: It's not sadness.
Calling it sadness is a FUCKING insult. It's DESPAIR.
Nothing left. 'Nowhere left to go but up'? Bullshit.
Nowhere left to go – period.

. . . Your coming to understand your loved-one's
painful situation is completely on the right track.
To those in that place, it is the only relief. They
are at their end. They have no more resources left
with which to battle, to 'maintain' . . . And so they
give themselves the only relief left. They know how
painful it will be for all those left behind, but they are
powerless to do otherwise. They simply cannot suffer
through it for one more day . . . one more hour . . . one
more minute.

The emails kept me going for a while because they helped
make sense of Rob's death at a time when nothing made
sense. I felt like I was lying at the bottom of the ocean, looking up at the surface awash in gold but unable to reach it, cut
off from everything, remote and dark, trying to fathom out
everything that had happened.

Why? Why did he do this?

Rob didn't leave a note; I pieced together his last words
from a patchwork of the conversations he had with those he
called and texted as he was fleeing the earth.

Only 30 per cent of people who die by suicide leave notes,

and, even then, the note doesn't provide absolution or truly explain what can never be explained: what was it that compelled the person to carry out an act that every part of our biology is created to fight against?

What I realised fairly quickly was that there were parts of Rob that made me feel like I didn't know him: the addiction, the lying, and how he handled his illness.

But I also knew Rob, I mean really knew him – better than anyone. And I knew that for this person, who loved so many people, who was loved by so many people, to finally not find any hope or happiness in the days to come, and to have struggled so long to stay alive, it must have been a state unimaginable.

When I called Prof. Williams about his book *Cry of Pain*, he said: 'When you get an inkling of the desperation of somebody, the emotional pain is as bad as a physical pain and coupled with the idea that this is going to go on forever, and there's nothing I can do about it, and my life has been irreversibly damaged by it and there's nothing left for me. And in that state, suicide seems like a blissful freedom. A real sense of freedom.

'In that book I talk about someone who meant to kill himself and was only saved by a complete accident, and he described to me graphically how, in those last few hours and minutes, he felt so at peace. When he suddenly realised he had the courage now, to take this step.'

Courage is a word people don't tend to use when it comes

to suicide. Instead, the word they use is selfish. And the worst phrase of all: 'Easy way out'.

Living is bloody hard, but making the choice to die is harder. Maybe the people who say it is easy are the lucky ones, because clearly they have never struggled so badly that they'd consider death. I mean, that Rob felt like that so much of the time, even on a sunny day when he was walking Daisy? How did he even survive as long as he did? That's not weakness, that's courage, no matter the outcome.

I spoke to Jonny Benjamin, who tried to jump off Waterloo Bridge in 2008. At the time he was struggling with being gay, and he has schizoaffective disorder, which is a combination of schizophrenia and depression. As he stood on the bridge, he was talked down by a man named Neil Laybourn, who convinced him to go for a coffee. Before they could actually do that, the police intercepted them and Jonny was sectioned. He didn't know Neil's name or how to get hold of him.

Six years later, he launched a campaign called 'Find Mike' – which he thought Neil's name was – to thank him for that act of kindness. It led to Jonny becoming a mental health campaigner and speaking widely about suicide prevention.

Jonny said: 'Throughout the whole journey on that bridge, I prayed for my family. "I don't want them to feel guilty," I kept on pleading to God. I had come to feel like a burden on them after becoming mentally ill and ending up in hospital. I believed it was better for all our sakes if I ended my life. The mental torture was too much to continuously bear and I truly thought I could never recover.'

People never get to choose how the ones they love die, but suicide will fool you into thinking that you could have done. And when someone you love takes their own life, every possibility held in the future torments you.

A number is attributed to everything. The number of kisses you had. The times you had dinner together on a Tuesday night. The times they held you when you cried, when you screamed at each other, laughed together. All of the firsts bookended by all of the lasts. Somewhere there is an inventory of your lives together and a number set against it, and the fact that the other person chose to end it can be the hardest thing to reconcile.

Much of the anger surrounding someone who killed themselves stems from the paradox that we believe the person had a choice, and made the choice to fuck over everyone they love on the way out. Prof. Williams echoed that. 'A lot of people are very angry . . . It's like a soldier leaving their post, which is a very ancient idea from some of the Greek philosophers. Feeling let down. It's a short step from believing, "This is the ultimate step that any of us can take" to thinking, "It's a selfish step, it's self-serving, and not thinking of others."' The reality, of course, is that by the time a person has reached the point where they fully intend to go through with suicide, they are doing so because they believe there are no other choices. And that everyone left behind will be better off without them.

He continues: 'I try to explain that in this sort of state you lose the sense of belief, the intentions and desires of other people. It's such a tunnel vision state in that what tends to go is what impact you might have on other people.

'It's just not in your cognitive state any more. It does not compute. It's like a module has been turned off. And we don't know because the research can't get at those last few moments, but it is . . . part of the condition that you lose the sense of the impact on other people. So I think society needs to try to find a way of being more forgiving about it.'

Forgiveness is an apt word. How do you even start to find out the why, when you feel like no one else wants to know, or worse, pretends like suicide doesn't exist?

In my search for more answers, I went on Rob's computer. I found solace in the most normal things, the completely mundane, such as his to-do lists.

Get quote about light fitting in office
Bloodworms for axys!
Move Poo's stuff out of the loft
Clean aquarium

But then I came across this, and realised it was the closest we would ever get to a suicide note.

[To Dr _____ , February 2014]

I feel all right today, but I've had periods of several days in a row where I think about suicide absolutely constantly, and I certainly have suicidal thoughts every day. It sometimes feels like a safety net, something I can rely on when I need it.

I have terrible insomnia, but I want to be asleep all the time because being unconscious is so much more attractive than being awake.

Faced with the prospect of living the rest of my life, the option of suicide is an attractive one. I generally feel that if it is going to be the case because of my depression that I face spending a significant amount of my time feeling the way I do, regardless of whether things are going well or badly, and regardless of, for example, my absolutely amazing and wonderful wife, suicide seems a viable alternative to being that down.

As has always been the case with my experience of depression, feeling low comes regardless of whether things are good or bad. It must be the case that ordinary people don't generally experience feeling the way I feel, I know it's not right to feel so incredibly bad, but it appears inescapable.

I could go on but you get the picture. I don't feel the

meds are currently effectively impacting on depressive feelings occurring in my brain regardless of external situations.

I would say I have on the three or four occasions I've described not gone so far as to make suicide attempts per se, but that said if I do go through with it – which I don't want to, for my wife and family's sakes apart from any-thing else – then I won't fail in the attempt. It is carefully planned.

I would hope, however, that they would understand that even a day or two of feeling the way I have been feeling for every single second of that day is unbearable.

We call suicide weakness. We say it is selfish. We say it's the easy way out.

But people who have reached that point have been fight-ing the hardest of fights for a long time. They have often been doing it on their own, because we don't respect or value people who are struggling inside their own heads. They are lost in their own battlefield and perhaps suicide is when it has become terminal. They cannot see the day when they won't be fighting. They are so very tired of fighting.

Whatever the outcome, we should be in awe of their life. We should get on our knees and honour the bravery and courage they had to stay in the world as long as they did, feeling as they did. We should remember their strength, not view them through a permanent prism of despair and sadness because of the manner in which they left it.

Immediately after Rob died, we barely had the energy to nod our heads at the tiny white cross that bore his name, a temporary marker until we chose a headstone. I ran my hands on the gold engraving, feeling the letters beneath my fingertips, closing my eyes against the new reality we had found ourselves in.

Nine months later, Prue, David and I decide to pick the headstone together.

Steve, the headstone guy who operates from a small industrial estate near Schnapper Rock, the cemetery where Rob is buried, is a mine of information. First, the stone comes not from local quarries, but from China. Steve even goes to a Stone Fair, which throws up a mind-boggling array of questions. I mean, in the hotel bar after a long day ogling quartz and dolomite, what would the conversation be like?

'Oh, the other day, I handled a *really* interesting hunk of granite,' someone would say, waggling their eyebrows.

Steve is extremely patient as we ask him many questions.

We consider engravings of kōwhai, a native New Zealand tree that takes over the landscape with brilliant yellow blossom in spring, after the pohutukawa's red blooms have finished.

My concerns are mainly centred around lettering, something Rob would have found hilarious, having mocked my interest in fonts yet still buying me books on typography. And then I think, *This is so wrong. He wouldn't have found it hilarious because he's dead. And his parents should not be here picking their son's headstone.*

I look at them moving up and down the aisles filled with stone where a son should be. They seem so small with this weight of grief upon their shoulders. I think of how much they have gone through, what they continue to go through. And there is such rage. I have never been angry at Rob for taking his own life because I understand, insofar as I can, how much pain he was in.

But I am angry at the collateral damage that has become our lives. I am angry when I think of the things we had to do, and continue to do. I am angry that his parents, whom I love, have to endure this when they should be on a cruise or starting a road trip to somewhere new and exciting.

Maybe it's the smell of granite in the morning, but after about an hour of fairly emotionless headstone talk, my fists clench and I realise the full implication of what we are doing and why we are there.

Rob is dead. And he is never coming back.

When Mal and I were in the airport on our way to Rob's funeral, I surreptitiously Googled 'how to cope with grief when you lose a spouse'.

I came across an account from a woman who said: 'At the

beginning, I focused on trying to get through the next six months, and my goal would be to make it alive at the end of that time.'

I remember thinking, *Wow, what a drama queen. I mean, 'staying alive' was her goal? As if it's that hard.*

What I didn't realise then was that I was in the pink cloud of shock. I was on autopilot, trying to get things done. A week after the funeral, I managed to cancel Rob's phone accounts, sort out the paperwork for his pension; I told his creditors to go fuck themselves and tied up all the loose ends around his invoices in half a day.

When the pink cloud wore off, it took me six months to cancel his Twitter account. It took fourteen months before I was able to go through his things and sort out what I'd keep and what would go to charity.

The irony of grief caused by suicide is finding the will to stay alive.

Two months after Rob died, I watched a film about the apocalypse and I realised, with a bit of a shock, that I would be relieved if I was wiped off the planet. I recognised I had turned a corner ten months later, when I knew I would actually be mildly concerned about surviving.

But I still have days where I could take living, or leave it.

Hoping to survive to the end of the week/month/year sounds incredibly self-indulgent and dramatic, but the exhaustion of grief is based on not knowing how you will feel from one moment to the next, feeling every spectrum of emotion at the same time, and believing this will never end.

You are in this world, but you don't belong to it. I was very lucky in that all of my friends got it – how to talk to me, what to say. But they couldn't protect me from everyone, from the hairdresser who told me I'd find someone else to the colleague who compared my loss to her cat dying. (FYI, pet death comparisons happen to widows and widowers a lot. I don't give a fuck if you're Noah and your entire ark died from foot and mouth, IT'S NOT THE SAME.)

Although people don't mean to, sometimes they make things worse. Some – including close family – didn't actually talk to me about Rob's death, or say they were sorry to hear about him to my face. When I vented to my mother about it – who had uncomplainingly absorbed a lot of the anger around my grief – she tried to calm me down by saying sometimes people weren't good with stuff like this.

'You know what, Mum, if someone's husband or wife died and I couldn't get over my own awkwardness to say: "I'm really sorry, are you okay?" then you should reconsider how you raised me.'

Not talking about Rob made him and my grief feel invisible. Those people who made things better were the ones who listened, told stories about him, made me laugh, and didn't say things like 'Stay positive' and 'You have to move on'.

That's not to say I was a dream when people did ask me

how I was. Rob's addiction, and the lies I had to tell around it, removed any last bit of artifice I had left. So the answers sometimes weren't what people expected, or wanted, to hear.

'How are you?'

'I'm fucking shit.'

'Oh.'

There were a lot of contradictions. I was so full of love for Rob, compassionate that he was no longer suffering. But I was also resentful that I had spent so long dealing with his addiction and depression, and I was now a widow trapped in further hell indefinitely. I appreciated the support my loved ones gave me, but I punished them for their concern.

I wanted to be left alone, I wanted to be smothered. I wanted everyone to suffer when they stopped posting updates about Rob on Facebook and got on with their lives, but I wanted good things to happen for them. I couldn't imagine being with anyone else but I was scared of being lonely for the rest of my life.

'I'm worried,' I said to my friend Has, who had moved in with me after Rob died, 'that I will never again love like that, or be loved like that.'

'Poo,' she replied, 'some people will never know what it's like to have a big love like that. And maybe you won't ever feel like that about anyone again. But you got to know what that kind of love feels like at least once in your life, and maybe that will have to be enough.'

At any rate, there was no space for anyone apart from Rob.

I was in love with a ghost, which suited me because I felt like I didn't belong with the living anyway.

Apart from those unavoidable moments before I went to sleep and immediately after I woke up, I flung myself into exercise. I signed up to a 10K to raise money for CALM, which meant training about three times a week. I found running so peaceful. I felt the wind braid my hair into knots, and once my lungs and heart adjusted and stopped screaming, 'WHAT ARE YOU DOING TO US!' everything took on slow, careful importance.

I knew the river's winding curves, the point where trees created a canopy across her edges, the bridges she sloshed against. And, when I made it into town, the London Eye, St Paul's and the Houses of Parliament framed in silhouette along her body.

My favourite route was near where I lived, and by the time I warmed up jogging from my house, I'd reach the bridge that took me into Richmond on the side of the river I liked running along. During my run I passed people enjoying pints in the sun, teenagers with bowed heads making a fumbling, foal-like entry into love, families stuffing ice creams into their mouths, and when I made my way back, I paused at the top of the bridge.

I could have had the best run of my life. The sun could be warming my face – a small pleasure I loved because it made me feel glad to be alive. I could have had a smile from a stranger that made me smile back.

But for a long time, I would always have a moment when I looked at the water below and thought about jumping in. Just to give me peace, just to end feeling like this, this relentless grief, this pain stitched into my chest. And for a second, I felt like I was speaking the language Rob wrote his last few moments in.

I saw the despair. I saw the hope it might end. I saw an endless sleep. And for a moment, I wanted it. Not the actual dying part, but the abnegation of self, the lack of existing, because if I didn't exist, I wouldn't feel like that.

And then I'd look away, and keep jogging. I'd look up at the sky and see how beautiful it was, a blue egg blown through with puffs of white clouds.

I'd jog all the way home. I'd stretch my calves while holding on to the crumbling brick wall. I'd notice how pretty my street was in summer, the magnolias dropping fat pink petals, the tenacious ivy eating my house.

I'd wipe the sweat off my nose, dig out keys from a back pocket.

I'd take a shower and smell that fresh goodness from my favourite soap.

These things, tiny as they may be, were enough to pull me back into the land of the living. But imagine that moment on the bridge stretched into an entire lifetime.

I couldn't bear it.

When I was back in the present, I knew time had passed. The light and warmth crept back in. I put my hand over my heart and felt it thump, and remembered the moment in hospital when I heard it talking to me through the echo, and how hard it had fought to keep me alive.

So even though I didn't understand how I was going to make it to a week, let alone a month, something told me that I was made of strong stuff.

And I knew that somewhere inside, despite the moment on the bridge that promised the gift of oblivion, I wanted to live.

*Felicity's house, where I am staying during my trip to New Zealand nine months after Rob's death, is near a beach called Narrow Neck, a small but pristine stretch of golden sand that presses out towards a clear horizon.*

*We have a routine. Early in the morning, regardless of how much wine we've had the night before, Felicity walks her dog Finbar along the beach during the short window when dogs are allowed on there. They return with Finbar freckling her wooden deck with drops of seawater and, shortly afterwards, I head out for a run.*

*The best time to run along Narrow Neck is first thing in the morning, before the tourists descend from the Devonport ferry. The beach is framed by a hill, along which cars zip up and down, making their way to the city, and I start my descent from the top, taking in the view of the beach.*

*Narrow Neck and I have a history. The day after Rob's funeral, I laced up my trainers and went for a run. I think people were surprised, but I felt that in times when nothing made sense, when the order of life as I knew it was chaos, I needed to keep doing the things that were simple and true.*

*It was the first time I'd run near Felicity's house, and I wasn't going in any particular direction when I came across the beach. Empty, quiet, no dogs; just the sea and the light pressing its fingers against the surface of the water.*

*I stopped. I looked at the waves summoning themselves into beautiful shapes flickering in the foam. I imagined him in the shift and turn of water, and I spoke to Rob for the first time since he died, without anyone else around. It was a poem of grief; it was a call to the skies for him to return.*

*In Hinduism, the practice of* sati *derives from the goddess Sati, who was so overcome with sadness because her father would not accept her husband, the god Shiva, that she burst into flames. And although the grief Shiva felt afterwards was colossal, and with him being one of the three most powerful gods there were terrible consequences, Sati was already being reborn into Parvati, the goddess of love and divine strength.*

*As I spoke to Rob's soul, I felt the oldness of the earth pass through me. Grief that arises from death is fire, and in this fire you will be remade into something different, something that feels and sees much deeper than other people around you. I was everything, and I was nothing.*

*When I return nine months later, one of the first things I do is to go for a run and stand where I stood before, to feel Rob on the horizon. I search the skies and the waves, but he isn't there.*

*I go back again and again, but I can't find him. He has dissolved into the ether, and like those beautiful shapes in the foam, he will never again take form. The sensation of loss is so sharp, it almost knocks me over.*

*I take my trainers off. I roll up my leggings. There is no one on the beach.*

*I walk towards the water, and I feel it swirl around my calves.*

*I am a girl, a woman, a wife. I am bones, I am blood, I am a soul. I am caught between two places – one lit in flames and the other radiating strength.*

*And just when I think I can't bear it any longer, when I feel like I am going to ignite from sadness, there is a voice that speaks. It struggles to cut through the tears and the hopelessness but it speaks.*

*I am so sorry this happened to you. You didn't deserve it.*
*I am sorry life let you down.*
*I will try to keep you up.*
*Remember I am here.*
*Always.*
*I will hold you up.*
*I will be strong.*
*Even when it seems like I'm not there,*
*I am.*
*I'm just tiny.*
*But I can grow. And I can*
*Carry both of us.*
*Remember.*

*And it's not Rob. And it's not God. That voice is mine.*

# Chapter Twelve

Here is what I knew about Rob before I went to New Zealand.

I knew he had left home when he was a teenager to live with his aunt Gabrielle after falling out with his parents. The picture that was painted was one of a child pushing the boundaries of what he could get away with, gradually spiralling out of control against a backdrop of strict parenting, until he left for Australia.

When he was twenty-one, his best friend Brendan Arnold passed away. It devastated him – they were like brothers – and he soon left for England, where he remained until shortly before his death. During his time in England, he had a large number of friends, he was well liked and well loved, and in the midst of this he lost a very close friend to a heroin overdose, Ben.

That gives you a certain chronological framework for who Rob was, but it doesn't tell you who he *actually* was.

The man I knew was complex, so complicated in fact that trying to unpick what was good, bad, beyond his control and downright shitty behaviour is impossible.

The man I fell in love with was gruff. He was kind. He could be aloof.

He went from having no degree to becoming a respected journalist. He built his garden with his own two hands, he bought his house with his own labour. He liked buying me flowers. He helped my friends when they needed manual labour done around the house. He cooked dinners for his friends when their loved ones died.

He had a unique sense of humour, mostly dry, observant and intelligent; goofy when he was trying to cheer me up. Our ability to bring levity to even the most horrendous shit got us through the dark times. This never waned even when he was in withdrawal, at the hospital or when we were stuck in a car park for eight hours trying to escape a festival.

When I told my parents we wanted to get married after about six months of dating, they asked me: 'What is it about him?'

'He makes me laugh and he's super-clever,' I said simply.

If you ask Jesse, the picture is the same but it's also less blinkered. He describes Rob as a wild man. 'You felt like you were on a ride going at one hundred miles per hour.'

I always believed the thing I loved about Rob was the stability he offered, but I think I was in complete denial. Of course, I loved his wildness; this man of earth and sea, who drew us all in with his intense contradictions.

But I don't think I ever properly recognised that the highs of being in love with a wild thing are always accompanied by the greatest of lows: when you want them to stop, to be tame alongside you, they can't.

Although Dr Shanahan helped me to see that Rob's lying was always around his addiction, and never about anything else, I don't know if I can fully reconcile the things that made me fall in love with Rob with the parts that lied and manipulated.

Was the drug Rob's wife and I was the affair? Rob would have hated such a statement because he thought he was better than that. But however much he hated it, it was the reality.

In the end, he lost his job, Daisy, me, the house – all of it.

The man I knew, who had fought for a semblance of normal life, would not willingly have let that happen, so what does it tell us about the fact that it did?

When I went over to New Zealand for the funeral, his brother John and I talked a lot. Poignantly, this would be the start of a relationship between us that was not possible when Rob was alive, because the two of them didn't get on.

'I felt when we came over for your wedding in 2011,' he said, 'we were presented with this version of Rob we'd never seen before. Well behaved, respectable. Once wild, now tame. I mean, was that *really* him?'

Sifting what was real and what wasn't is a daunting task.

But I do know that other people's accounts make me reassured that the best parts I loved about him were also what they loved about him.

When I asked Jesse about his favourite time with Rob, he said it was when they went to Grenada together in 2008, the island where Jesse's family is from.

'It was my first time ever going there, and Rob was a big reason I ever went in the first place. He lectured me quite a bit about knowing my homeland and not being a real West Indian until I went there. And what a lovely and insane two weeks we had.

'Every day was the same: Rob would wake up early – I'd sleep in until noon. I'd find him in the garden, shirtless, taking pictures of butterflies and lizards. He'd cook breakfast. We'd go down to the beach. We'd swim and chill for hours.

'Then I'd start watching horrible original sci-fi movies, while Rob sat next to me, reading for hours and hours.

'Every so often he'd look up from his book and tell me something about cricket, or spiders, or how on islands it's especially important to conserve water and I was doing the dishes wrong and I really should be more earth conscious, or tell me that I had horrible taste in television, or inform me how he was going to get darker than me from the sun.

'We all know how much Rob wished he was a brown person.'

Our last overseas holiday together was in India in 2014,

where we gathered for my cousin's wedding. Rob had been clean for two months. I had been worried about his behaviour but he was superb – the guy I fell in love with had returned. When we weren't running around doing wedding-related stuff or meeting relatives over dosas and chicken curry, we had an easy, sleepy routine while based in my parents' modern flat in Bangalore.

In the guest room where we stayed, there was a balcony overlooking the rest of the street, where he sat smoking cigarettes while having his first ever pedicure. He had been ordered to by Mum after she caught a glimpse of the thick crusts of hard skin underneath.

The reason why he had acquired these hobbit feet became evident a few weeks before, when Rob went to Sainsbury's without shoes on and I only realised when I saw someone staring at his bare feet.

'JESUS CHRIST!' I yelled. 'Where the HELL are your shoes?'

He shrugged. When I saw people walking around without shoes in the supermarkets in New Zealand and was told it was a Kiwi thing, it made more sense.

Rob wore his lungi every day and would walk around the neighbouring streets, making sure he visited the tiny Ganesh temple and talked to his new friend 'Swamji', the priest who ran the place. He spotted fruit bats from the balcony, and spied a cuckoo in the trees.

He even made friends with the guy at the end of the

street whose job it was to fold used paper and sell it on for a pittance at the recycling plant. This person, probably at the lowest end of the economic chain, assumed Rob was a white hobo due to the lungi and vest, and offered to lend him some clothes.

In the middle of this familiarity and family life, our drug secret was ever present. We had to pay a visit to the dentist because Rob's teeth were rotting and crumbling in his own mouth because of his heroin use.

To try to understand the full truth of Rob makes me fearful that the man I married was a stranger. And if the only thing I ever knew was real was that he loved me, who was the person I fell in love with?

Rob was born in December, a chubby little thing with light brown hair, big blue eyes and cheeks so fat Gabrielle nicknamed him Bobble.

It was 1975 in Auckland. Cicadas were calling summer into existence, doors and windows were flung open to press against the heat, fizzy sodas crackled in plastic tumblers on wooden decks and pohutukawas were beginning their slow march from dark green foliage into stiff red blossoms, shooting flames against a blue sky.

In other parts of the world, 1975 saw Margaret Thatcher become the leader of the Conservative Party in opposition, the first woman to lead a major political party in the UK, and, on a bigger scale, the Vietnam War came to an end. The world ended and remade itself as it did every year, with an equal measure of wonder and horror.

But on 23 December, infinite potential was held in those blue eyes, as it is for every newborn. Safe, smelling of milk, swaddled in blankets. Future loves, triumphs, failures waiting in the wings in the burning glow of new life.

Baby Bobble ate, slept, pooped his way to being a toddler, and a couple of years later John came along with his shock of blond hair, and after that came Alan, looking exactly like his father.

Rob's birthdays were celebrated with cake, parties and paper hats. Toothy Rob is captured in a photograph where he will live now forever, with arms planted on his hips, smiling at the camera, surrounded by cousins and friends thrust into shorts and t-shirts.

When he wasn't tracing pictures of animals and plants with his friend Mark Gilbert, he was obsessing over geckos and skinks. There were cages, the specialist food they needed to eat. Memorised notes of every species of gecko and skink that existed in New Zealand. It explained a lot about his later acquisitions of the axolotls, salamanders and newts.

When he was growing up in 1980s Auckland, Prue and David were pretty strict practitioners of their faith but have since softened, in part due to their own humanist beliefs clashing with dictates of the Church.

Boy Rob played the violin. He was perfectly behaved. He

went to the Junior Naturalists' Club with his mother, who studied botany and instilled in him a love of plants and the way the planet worked. He got his love of classical music from his father, who worked as an accountant.

There are pictures of a young, bespectacled Rob with long, lanky legs, a mop of brown hair, bright blue eyes and this beautiful smile.

I asked Mark, a close family friend who had known him since he was four and who described their time in the Junior Naturalists as them being 'animal nerds', to tell me what Rob was like. They were born hours apart and shared their birthdays every year when growing up.

'Clever. Nerdy. He was always the most observant person in the room and I was always a bit jealous of it. We played at each other's houses a lot with Lego, *Star Wars* toys, cricket and making mud in their back garden.

'He was a huge influence on me. We were competitive, or I was comparing, and there were lots of times I think I felt a bit in his shadow.'

Mark said Rob had a wonderful imagination, and wrote stories even when he was at primary school. 'One was going through the jungle in South America – that was the first time I heard of an anaconda. Another was a Western mystery.'

Somewhere between nine and eleven, Rob was being bullied by older boys. He told me once, in tears, when he was trying to piece together why his brain worked the way it did. 'Why can't I let it go?' he said. 'Why do I keep going back to it, every detail of it, when it's been years? Why did they do that?' I looked at his tears and I clenched my jaw.

My sadness for the little boy who still lived within this man, who had some of the sweetness and inquisitiveness pummelled out of him, was being burned off by the rage I felt. I was Kali, limbs of indigo blue, bringing death, destruction and wildness against these little shits who had hurt him, stringing their skulls into necklaces and drinking their blood like wine.

Bullying makes a child feel worthless. When you consider a child who is bullied and factor in depression – which can start as early as seven – I imagine the consequences to be immense. Rob believed that his depression started very young, and when it did begin to cause problems for him the circumstances were not in his favour.

Towards the end of the eighties, the Bell family had a lot on. David's parents died within a year of each other. His sister had terminal cancer. Prue was doing everything she could to keep things afloat, and I cannot imagine it was easy with three young boys. There wasn't a great deal of attention to go around with such seismic shifts taking place.

Meanwhile, Rob was making the transition that we all do, from the safe confines of primary school to the edgier world of secondary school. Not adults but not fully children either, play-acting with emotions we didn't fully understand, some lucky not to get hurt, others acquiring wounds that would stay with them for life.

The bullying would have undermined the things Rob loved – all of the science stuff, playing the violin, the passionate attention to detail about the skinks – and one of his friends, Louise Russell, said that Kiwi boys could be pretty rough at that age. She and Rob met when he was eleven, and she described him as 'pretty weedy looking – I remember he had really skinny legs and these very geeky-looking square-framed glasses'.

On the first day of class, Rob's teacher asked if anyone had vision or hearing issues who might need to sit up the front.

Louise said: 'Rob didn't volunteer but I clearly remember her asking him to move up the front since he was wearing glasses. So he ended up sitting next to me. My first impression of him was of an incredibly angry person. He was fuming, I think, at being singled out for wearing glasses.

'I said hi and introduced myself as he sat down, and he just folded his arms and pursed his lips and stared straight ahead.'

Louise witnessed him being bullied verbally in that first year, along with a bit of pushing and shoving, but Rob was already learning to change. By the end of that year, he had started smoking and, while still friends with the nerdy people he had arrived with, was starting to seek out cooler people.

'The way he was when I first met him,' Louise continued, 'he acted like someone who had his armour on, who was expecting a beating to come – it was nearly thirty years ago and yet I remember his demeanour so clearly.

'The fact he was super-brainy and looked like a nerd would have, I'm quite certain, made it inevitable that he was a target for bullies. I bet it all stopped as soon as he started growing, though. By the end of third form he was pretty tall and starting to fill out.'

In that first year, though, something happened that shook their entire class. A classmate, Chris Davies, fell off the back of a milk truck and died. Louise said it was handled really badly; they weren't offered any counselling and, for her personally, it sparked a bout of depression and destructive behaviour.

'I don't remember how he dealt with it at the time, but knowing him as I do I suspect it might have fucked him up a bit as it did me.'

Something I didn't know about Rob until a year before he died: he was predisposed to self-harm. Very early on in our relationship, I noticed scars at the top of his arm, something that looked like words deeply carved in. I ran my finger over the skin.

'What's this?' I asked with concern.

'Oh, nothing.'

'Rob, these look pretty bad.'

'I'd rather not talk about it.'

Was this what that armour was made of? Carved from his own flesh? Did any of us realise the price it had cost him?

When I was a teenager, I remember self-harm was this really emo way of saying 'I'm fucked up' when you weren't. Some girls would come in with superficial cuts and show them off to each other, and then in a moment the phase passed and we forgot about it.

But beneath the superficiality, there were people for whom this was real. It wasn't a phase. When we were fledgling adults, a close friend of mine eventually revealed why she always wore long sleeves at school. She showed me: like flesh-coloured bangles pressed hard against the skin, a knife wielded like a pen, writing the pain into ribbon upon ribbon of scar tissue.

Rob's cuts got deeper as he got older, and he spoke about his depression to friends like Louise.

Although their friendship started in an inauspicious way on that first day when he was bristling with fury, he went on to become one of her closest friends and confidants, even when he changed schools.

'At a time when we were all so awkward with our bodies, I loved that Rob would wrap everyone – boys or girls – in a giant bear hug,' she said. 'He would be warm and affectionate and there was no sexual undertone.'

By this age, Gecko Rob was rapidly becoming a distant memory. He was struggling to come to terms with who he was, but he had somehow fashioned a coat of confidence that he wore permanently. This would be the beginnings of that swagger, slow drawl and air of seeming nonchalance.

At its worst points, it would manifest as obnoxiousness, attention-seeking.

At fifteen he went to Rosmini College, where he became part of this large, swirling group of friends – genuinely good people and mostly from good families – who listened to punk and metal. At this stage, Rob was messing around with alcohol and pot, but probably not much more than most teenagers and the group he hung around in.

He grew his hair long – something that didn't go down well at home – and started to wear Doc Martens and a long trench coat. There was no doubt that his striving to fit in, his evolution as one of the cool gang, was straining his relationship with his parents, who wanted him to behave. They didn't understand why this was happening; he felt they didn't understand him and were trying to control him.

That push and pull between a highly conservative atmosphere at home and nineties naughtiness was unravelling their previously perfect relationship to a damaging degree. A significant moment of him asserting his own rights was his refusal to go to church.

So Rob the wonder child morphed into a living nightmare. He smoked, he drank. He cut school, he listened to rock music. So far, so teenager, but it was edgier than that, I gather.

Prue and David's rejection of Rob's ongoing rebellion and his refusal to conform, in any way, to their rules or expectations created such a toxic atmosphere that he went to stay with Gabrielle.

It seemed, then, that he began detaching himself from his parents. If they asked him to do something, he'd refuse to do it – even if he didn't feel that strongly about it. And certainly the one quality that drove me mad about Rob was what he called his 'contrariness'.

'If someone is asking me to do something,' he said to me once, puffing his chest out, 'I'm just not gonna wanna do it.' He sounded about fifteen.

'Rob, I don't give a fuck. Just do the dishes, because if you don't, I'll have to.'

We didn't fight often, but the phrase I used most often was: 'I'm not your mum. You are a grown adult in a grown-up relationship.'


Despite his great intelligence, he dropped out of school at sixteen and undertook a variety of jobs, from shearing at a sheep station to working as a bartender, driving trucks to landscape gardening.

'I dropped acid, drank twenty-four cans of beer and drove a truck I didn't have a licence for,' he once told me with pride.

I didn't tell him it sounded beyond stupid – I knew how clever he was and it seemed baffling he had thrown that potential away. But this was history with clearly a lot of unresolved pain that he had refashioned into some anarchist existence.

Although Rob would never go into any great detail about

his childhood, beyond that he rebelled and had left home, it was evident to me that he was depressed as a child, and did not realise it at the time.

Plenty of children have to do battle with strict parents and do not end up going down the same path he did. And Prue and David didn't seem strict in an Amish sort of a way – like toiling in the fields and shunning electricity. They seemed strict in more of an Indian sense – our grandmother, for instance, forbade us to watch *Thriller* (so we waited until she fell asleep).

To me, it suggests something else was going on, something that neither Rob nor his parents were equipped to deal with.

It's a common pattern for children who have mental health problems not to be able to articulate how they feel. And once they hit fourteen, what is a child's mental illness develops into an adult one, with adult symptoms. Adult rage. Adult despair. Adult chaos. However, it transmits without any of the experience, power or vocabulary of an adult because they aren't one.

A lot of people write this behaviour off as 'being a teenager', but what is actually being played out is the struggle of mental illness. These years are crucial in developing good coping mechanisms. But not enough is known about how to help children and parents through mental illness when it presents this young.

We're only just having a conversation about it now, and I

know several parents who are utterly lost when it comes to dealing with their kids who have mental health issues. The immense guilt they feel is not fair – this is a much bigger problem than they have the capacity to deal with. It is exactly as if their child has been diagnosed with a heart condition and they are expected to cure them without help.

A 2008 study said that 10 per cent of children have a diagnosable mental illness (this could start as young as five) but only 70 per cent of these ended up getting intervention at an early age. What chance did Rob and his family stand in 1985, when the prevention and treatment of adult mental illness was still experimental? When, thirty years later, with regard to children's mental health, it is still in its infancy?

In some ways, although we grew up on different continents and had a five-year age gap, parts of his adolescence were not that different to mine, or other people who were into alternative music.

We tapped into it because we felt like we didn't quite belong in cookie-cutter suburbia. We romanticised death because our rock and roll idols did, we sought to emulate their pain in our safe, sanitised world of sandwiches with the crusts cut off.

Like him, I was also part of a social galaxy that constantly shifted and turned, friends making connections at parties, chance introductions that opened up worlds filled with other exciting people, music that blew our minds. All of us barely-there adults walking shakily on newly formed legs that tried to run before they could walk, intense friendships that blew hot at the centre of it all, people without whom we couldn't imagine an existence.

Louise spoke of the letters Rob wrote to her and other people, multiple pages of how he felt and what was going on in their universe. In Kent, 11,671 miles away, my friends and I did the same, sackfuls of letters filled with our darkest thoughts, scribbles of cocks and our intentions to shag/marry/kill whatever hapless male had walked into our orbit that month.

But here is where the similarities end. Plenty of kids get bullied. Lots mess around with drugs and alcohol. For some, there are pivotal traumas. But not all of them go on to become addicts.

For a person to go on to develop a lifelong problem with substance abuse, it isn't just about one story, one moment in time, any one person or the nuances of parenting, as long as the general environment was safe. Depression, when it occurs in teenagers, starts to manifest as an adult illness with adult symptoms. So anger, acting out (especially in boys) and behavioural problems.

Was this what Rob was going through?

For a person to never grow up beyond a certain point, and to always have one method of dealing with hardship, that hints at layer upon layer of personal struggle.

I remember John once saying to me: 'You know what I couldn't get over? That whenever I tried to have a conversation with Rob, he just couldn't move past being sixteen. He seemed permanently stuck at that age.'

Having witnessed Rob about to walk out on his mother during a conversation that wasn't a fight, when Prue had done nothing to warrant such an over-the-top, dramatic reaction, I knew what he meant, although, significantly, he had never been like that with me.

When I spoke to Mr B, my mental health source, about this, he said: 'So what happened to Rob at sixteen, which means when shit happened, he turned back into a stroppy teenager? Was it that when he was sixteen he wasn't heard or something he was feeling couldn't be expressed, so when he was feeling pressure, it was really difficult?

'And now, there are all sorts of things coming out about perfectionism and rumination. Do we want perfectionism from our kids, do we want perfect kids? Perfectionism layers so much stress and anxiety on young people, no wonder some explode or rebel, or use food as a means of control.

'So what did he not feel in control of, potentially, and what did he use as a means of gaining control? Was it drugs? Did they free him or give him control in the choices he made because no one was listening to him? Was he trying to say something? Did someone close to him die? Or did he just never learn to have a sense of social maturity?'

It is undeniable that he was going through more than

just being a teenager. The self-harm is the symptom of that struggle, even though we will never truly know what was in his head or how he processed things. All I know is that he found it very difficult to ask for help and, sometimes, he was in complete denial about his own reality and, without insight, could never properly get help.

Out of the friendship group Louise spoke about, most went on to have perfectly boring, normal lives with partners and kids. The only person who didn't – apart from Rob – was Brendan. Wesley referred to Brendan, Rob and himself as the three musketeers. They were part of that huge group of friends Rob met at Rosmini.

After Rob died, Wes looked broken, the last man standing, the other two having burned up like meteors entering the atmosphere too fast.

Rob told me about Brendan very early on in our relationship. He described him as a soulmate, the kind of relationship where you don't have to communicate with the other person verbally to know what they are thinking. He was still in love with him, years later, a friendship that affected him so deeply, a death he never totally recovered from.

They became friends at primary school, when Rob was in the Cub Scouts and Brendan's mother was their Cub Scout leader. I wish I could have met Brendan because, like Rob, he had that rare quality of not caring about a person's race or gender – if you were a good human that was more than enough. By all accounts, like Rob, he would also do anything for you; they'd both give you the shirt off their back – and I wonder who influenced who. There's no denying that Brendan helped Rob through some of his more difficult moments while growing up.

Perhaps at one point they were almost the same being, in the way that intense friendships have a way of melting and reforming you into one person who thinks, acts and talks the same way.

Brendan was into punk and ska, and so was Rob. They both dressed as skinheads, but the movement was not the same as it was elsewhere – at the end of the world, in New Zealand, it was more about the fashion and music, and not about politics and fascism.

They grew up together, in each other's pockets, but around the time they turned twenty the picture becomes unclear. Brendan went to Scotland, where he passed away. At this juncture, Rob was still on 'softer' drugs like alcohol and weed, although some people say that he was abusing alcohol quite heavily. Anecdotally, from certain things Rob told me, I know this to be the case. But he always framed it in a joke, or the swagger of an ex-smoker who was able to brag about how much they'd smoked because they didn't do that any more.

When they gathered for Brendan's funeral in New Zealand, Rob was a wreck. The other half of him had been torn away. There was some behaviour on his part that people didn't feel comfortable talking to me about, but I can imagine that in the most painful moment of his life, losing his closest friend at twenty-one probably prompted a severe bout of self-harm and alcohol abuse.

Shortly afterwards, Rob left New Zealand for good.

We all want to piece together the point at which we could have saved him. To find the thing or the person responsible so that it might make sense of his death or make our anger righteous. But there isn't such a thing.

Did Rob ever reach his own judgement? I remember over-hearing a conversation with his parents on Skype, in which he said: 'But I just want to be normal.' The tone was a child's tone. Not childish, but child-like. Upset, small, frightened.

And I heard Prue try to talk him through it, to make him see that he wasn't less of a person because he needed to take medication. 'You have to see it as a diabetic views insulin; this is just what you need to manage it.'

How can we ever really know what created Rob's problems, when he himself couldn't articulate the depth of them, or didn't want to acknowledge their existence to others? When admitting his depression, his self-harm – to his parents or teachers – would mean he was that little kid again, forced to sit at the front of the class because he was different?

There is a word that explains what I think Rob struggled with all of his life, despite the hundreds of friends and his ability to be loved by so many people. It is the thing that Jane

Powell from CALM alludes to when she is talking about the type of man who is most at risk of suicide.

It is a word we don't think of when it comes to these men because they are so busy creating noise and colour, distracting us with their confidence, so that we don't notice it. It is a word we didn't associate with Rob, who sometimes seemed so arrogant that he could fix it all himself, who belittled our concern for him.

I have no doubt that everything began and ended with this word.

'There's this poem that I memorised when I was a little kid,' Jesse told me when we were talking about Rob. 'It starts: "I never knew your loneliness, and knowing now, I die".'

*Loneliness.*

I'm not talking about going to the cinema on your own or buying meals for one. This is the kind of loneliness that kills – especially men, who cannot tap into their social networks in the same way women can. This is the kind of loneliness that comes about as a result of experiences that make you feel small and worthless, that you cannot articulate to anyone. That, as you grow older, becomes a way of living, a way of surviving. But it isn't, not even close.

Asking for help, kindness and human connection is one of the hardest things you can do, because not only does it mean opening yourself up, exposing your vulnerabilities, it also means putting your faith in other people. And sometimes people can be shitty, small-minded and let you down.

But in the end, not being able to ask for help is what killed Rob. It's killing so many of our young men.

Truly, among those of us who shared the closest moments with him, from giving birth to him to gifting him Daisy as a puppy, from his first kiss to his last one, none of us ever really knew Rob's loneliness.

When someone you love dies, they are a supernova.

For so long, they shone brightly in your world. When they self-destruct, the shockwaves shatter everything you know.

This person is now made of a million memories and atoms that float in the cosmos; everything they ever were is transforming into something altogether different.

You cannot see what is happening. The blast has rendered you dumb. You can only see the pieces of your life, the brightness that person used to be, and the blackness that now surrounds the space where they once existed.

The smoke clinging to their jacket. The sound of their voice alive only in data on your phone. Their favourite book that will never again be touched by their hands. These things will break your heart over and over again, until it feels like you will never get up.

But get up: because this is what is happening.

You aren't just saying goodbye to them, you are saying goodbye to yourself. The star was so powerful and beautiful, your love for them burned up the person you were.

This is how it is meant to be. And as they explode into stardust, when all we can see is their death, they are already once again becoming a part of life, from the first breath in a baby's mouth to the rain watering the ground.

*You are already changing, dear one. It is painful, and you don't want it. You want the fading light of your ghost and you can't bear their absence. But if you are lucky, the world won't let you go. It isn't your time yet.*

*So you slowly turn into something stronger. You realise what you have a choice over, and what you don't. You turn what you know into strength, you help others find theirs, and you are gifted a compassion that is so deep and limitless, at times it is the only thing that gives you peace.*

*You watch people scurry about in their lives. You see them worry about futures they arrogantly assume they have. They furrow their brows about getting older when you know each year is a gift.*

*They forget your loss, often, even though for you it is always the first thing you wake up with, and the last thing you hold close when you go to bed. You cannot go where they are going. But that's all right.*

*They aren't supposed to know what this feels like. Yet.*

*And, although for a while it feels like this is all there will ever be, you look down and see you are different. Your beloved is a part of you and always will be, and you finally see that leaving this earth will not reunite you or bring you peace.*

*The hope that each day will bring new strength, however tiny, and that a day or a week may come where you can carry your loss and your new life in your heart at the same time, is what keeps you going.*

# Chapter Thirteen

There is a big conversation gathering pace, about the problem with masculinity and how it is putting men in prison, pushing them towards substance abuse and killing them off.

In his documentary *All Man*, the artist Grayson Perry talks about why men are in jail, which I think can be applied to why they are in trouble in general: 'For the reasons that are classically male. They are proud, they are strong, they want to DO STUFF; they have to be the top dog. They don't want to change, they don't want to ask for help. They are young, and forever young in arrested development.'

Rob had depression and struggled with addiction, but I am in no doubt that the sense of masculinity he ascribed to also prevented him from properly acknowledging his problems and, most importantly, from being able to ask for help. The armour he created to become a man, in the end, shattered.

Although suicide is the biggest killer of men under

POORNA BELL

forty-five in the UK, and in the US men are four times more likely to complete suicide than women, there has never been a gendered study to find out why suicide rates are rising. Jane from CALM has been banging this drum for years, saying it 'beggars belief'.

'It is about guys and what we expect from guys. Slightly more women than men consider suicide, and yet they don't complete. The difference, as far as I can see, is that women feel able to say: "I'm suicidal, I need help." They have that door where they can ring for a friend.

'Men don't have that door because to say, "I need help, I'm vulnerable and I am hurting" would be to emasculate themselves. To not be a proper man. So what they feel is that they don't have that option. Rather than slitting their wrists and deciding at what point to call for help, they go for the quickest and most effective option because what could be worse than failing to kill myself? How pathetic would I be?'

If the things mostly likely to kill a man (and specifically not women) were road accidents, cancer or heart disease, could we honestly say there wouldn't be a massive push to find out why this was happening and then for every public body to show us how they are working towards prevention?

But there isn't. And although we can launch crisis centres and pump more money into mental health, we need to go a bit further back. Some hard questions need to be asked around what we expect from men, and, consequently, what they expect from themselves.

I mean, really, what did I expect from Rob?

As a feminist who fights daily for gender equality, I still expected him to take out the bins and pick up dog crap because it was a man's job. I expected him to do most of the grunt work when it came to moving house, and around bigger things I almost certainly (despite not wanting to admit it) expected him to be the breadwinner, and that he would be able to swoop in and take care of things when I needed him to.

Does this mean I was one of many people who trapped Rob in this narrow vision of what masculinity is? Undoubtedly. I may never have said 'man up', I may have given him love, support and a judgement-free space to conduct his recovery, but I was never going to push him to be different because I had learned what a man is from my dad, who learned it from his dad and his dad before him.

But maybe the more important question is what did Rob expect from himself as a man?

He believed it was the man's responsibility to look after things. To sort things out and be economically valuable. To be a good husband, which required providing safety and a house. There wasn't much room for softness or failure.

There were also so many contradictions. He was so self-assured in not giving a shit about what people thought. He said what he wanted, he wore what he wanted, and he wouldn't care if it made him look silly. Or if he hurt someone's feelings with his bluntness.

As an adult he went into raptures about water voles, delighted at spotting bitterns and doted over his colony of newts – the same interests he probably got bullied about as a kid in school. So that experience didn't turn him away from the things he loved, but it was almost as if the process of surviving the ordeal created something incredibly hard and inflexible around other aspects of his life.

In creating his armour he became this wild man, someone who didn't play by the rules, whip-smart, unpredictable yet gentle, kind and thoughtful towards people, but, in an instant, caught in the spiral of his own destruction.

When I asked him why he found it so hard to talk about his feelings, he blamed it on a long-ago ex-girlfriend of his who broke his heart and cheated on him. 'I wore my heart on my sleeve until then,' he said. But I don't know that I believe it, even though she did look like an asshole in the pictures I saw of her tucked away in a shoebox. I think it was an excuse.

So much of what he learned about the expectations of being a man would have begun long before this woman. And so much of his inability to open up wasn't the fear of getting hurt – it was the fear that, by doing so, he wouldn't measure up.

For someone to consistently not be able to ask for help, even when the stakes were so high – our marriage and our future – that to me speaks of entrenched, dysfunctional behaviour.

Jesse said: 'His bravado, strength of character and tough

"harden the fuck up" (to quote Rob himself) attitude wasn't something I had, or could have. But I think that might have been why he chose me to be friends with.

'Even how I was falling apart when I first met him, I think this vulnerability spoke to the vulnerability in him.

'When I asked Rob how he was feeling about this or that, he'd dodge me, he'd joke, he'd avoid answering or feeling exactly what was really happening. But he didn't expect the same of me – he was the best listener, the best comforter, the best advice giver.'

I think it was possible to be both 'fuck what the world thinks' and still be shackled to this rigid template of masculinity. However much of an anarchist he liked to think he was, Rob wasn't immune to it. In fact, if the toxic prison of modern-day masculinity is a virus, then he died of it.

Looking back now, there were flashes of what lay beneath the bravado. When he was yet again thousands of pounds in debt to creditors who knew he'd had problems paying it back before but didn't mind loaning it anyway, he felt pinned by shame and fear. First, that he'd got himself into that situation and, second, that he was relying on his wife to sort things out.

When we moved house for the second time, he was worrying about getting the cash together for the deposit.

'Don't worry,' I said, 'we'll use the deposit we get from the first place to pay for it.'

'And who paid that? Was it me?'

I nodded. 'Good,' he grunted. 'I managed to do that at least.'

The first time I tried to get him to come with me to the gym (it took three attempts until it stuck), I was so disappointed that his attendance tapered off.

After the third month of him paying for the membership but not using it, I lost it.

'WHY?' I asked.

For once he didn't say he was busy with work or that he hadn't slept well. He replied quietly: 'I just feel really intimidated in there. I don't feel comfortable asking anyone to help either.'

I didn't really know what to say, so I didn't say anything – but I realised how big a deal it was that he'd actually told me the truth about how he'd been feeling.

Perhaps the most revealing moment, however, was when we took Daisy to a kennel two weeks into our separation. With Rob in hospital and me out of the house for twelve hours of the day, she wasn't coping well home alone and needed proper care.

He cried most of the journey there, and most of the journey back. We were miserable sending our dog away even if it was just for a week, and miserable with each other. We wanted to be together but we couldn't be there for each other because we were separating.

Finally, I said: 'Rob, I just don't understand, honey. I know how much you love me. I know how much you want me in your life. Why, *why* couldn't you ask for help?'

He took his time replying but when he did, he said: 'Every time I reach that moment, I'm just a boy. I'm scared and I'm frightened and I feel really small. I know what I need to do, but . . . I can't. I just can't.'

Trying to grasp the real Rob is like looking at the edge of the shoreline and endeavouring to make sense of the waves. They shift all the time, making it impossible to sense the pattern and meaning in why and how they exist.

Suicide always brings it back to responsibility. Whose responsibility was he? Who was in charge of his life? And when you're feeling guilty, like you didn't do enough or say the right things, these questions are critical to restoring a sense of perspective.

Rob was an incredibly proud man. It's impossible to extricate the things he valued as a man, and the things he felt trapped by. His most admirable quality was doing things his own way. It was also his most frustrating quality because he thought he knew best and had everything in hand when he didn't.

You cannot impose your own will on someone like that – especially if you love them – and then expect them to retain their sense of honour and self-esteem.

But I know he had a problem with the silence that gagged men, even if, paradoxically, he felt bound by it too. 'We're expected to man up, suffer in silence and get on with it,' he once said. 'How did it ever work for our father's generation?' Well, it didn't – which explains why suicide rates among men are high in the over sixty-fives, and the terrible legacy of their masculinity is still affecting younger men.

Jane thinks that this idea that men can't communicate or say how they feel because that's how their gender is wired is balls.

'When you look at art, literature, music and poetry for the last few thousand years, and how much of that was produced by men, then it's complete nonsense.

'Guys will talk about stuff – they will never buy a tub of ice cream and talk for hours on the phone – but they *will* have conversations.'

In the search for answers about changing the conversation around mental health, Mr B told me that it wasn't just a question of de-stigmatising mental illness, or making it easier for guys to talk. It was about changing the entire approach to mental health.

He said we needed a three-pronged strategy. First, to promote good mental health – and, crucially, to encourage society to value this. Second, to tackle mental distress, in order to catch someone before it tips over into illness. Third, to amend how we treat mental illness, which needs better understanding and care.

'What if our view of mental health was different?' he said. 'Where we viewed good mental health as an asset, we encouraged people from the very point of preconception, to conception, having kids, school, work; where we become robust about dealing with mental health?'

Mr B said we have a whole profession dedicated to cat-egorising different behaviours, and it's built on observing, defining and treating these behaviours. He raises a very good point, which is that the main treatment involves alter-ing chemicals in the brain, but that this only addresses the symptoms, not the root cause. So for some people it works, for others – for instance, those who have PTSD after childhood abuse – it doesn't, because it doesn't tackle recovery in terms of dealing with the abuse itself.

His view – one that I agree with – is that we perceive mental illness as something to be fixed, and once someone is 'fixed' we expect them to be recovered. There is a much bigger picture than that, he argues, which is that if, culturally, we understood mental health and illness properly, then we would be better at treating it. This means appreciating the complexi-ties of the brain and how that links to someone's background, who they are and what shaped them, and understanding that there is no one-size-fits-all remedy.

There's a charity in the UK called Place2Be, of which the Duchess of Cambridge is a patron. They do an incredibly important job, which is to address the problem of mental health in children, to teach parents and educators to recognise and support these children with the overall goal of preventing them from going on to develop a mental illness when they are adults.

Their work draws fuel from a powerful statistic – 50 per cent of adult mental illness could have been prevented if people had been given the right support and treatment when they were a child.

They have a heavy task on their hands. Considering Rob would have struggled with depression when he was around ten or twelve, not much has changed in the last thirty years in terms of addressing mental health at a young age; parents still feel helpless and lost. They don't have the words or understanding to navigate this little-known territory and the worst part is that they aren't given any help to realise when things are going wrong.

'There's lots of research into how people treat boy and girl babies,' said Prof. Williams. 'So if you give someone a baby and tell them it's a girl, they speak to them differently than if it's a boy.

'What emerges is that with boys, conversation is much more instrumental than emotional. It's problem-solving rather than speaking about emotions. It may well be there are basic differences but, in a sense, children don't have a chance if even the way we relate to them is using different vocabularies.

'If men are better at being instrumental, they won't be talking about emotions. They will then be spared some of the more mild mental health issues [that young women have]. But given that they will have the same pressures as other people do, when they do break down, it will be a more catastrophic breakdown. Because there hasn't been the willingness to express what has been going on with their life.'

When I think about the expectations Rob had of himself – to be able to work full time, have children, be in a marriage, be the breadwinner, be the perfect son/son-in-law, be responsible and law-abiding, never cry, never show weakness, never be the one who could say: 'I can't do this' – no wonder he was exhausted.

'The expectations they have of themselves can't be fulfilled,' said Jane, 'they are impossible. And it's actually a large element of society that is totally unreasonable.'

When faced with only two narrow choices – either never really taking responsibility, or assuming the heavy, grotesque burden that male adulthood seems to entail – can we blame men for being fearful of growing up?

A month after Rob's funeral in Auckland, we held a memorial service for him in London, in his cousin Karen's house. Karen put together a slideshow of Rob's photos: him laughing, cuddling Daisy, sharing a beer, posing with nothing but strategically placed banana leaves (cut from his banana plant, of course). There were a lot of tears. A lot of laughter. A lot of beautiful things said.

But the thing that will stay with me was something his friend Jon Hess said. Jon is a wonderful musician, and I wanted him to sing at the memorial.

Before Jon sang that day, he spoke a few words. He said he'd always talked to Rob about his problems, and wished Rob had been able to talk to him. He also described how, the night before the memorial, he'd had a dream in which Rob was standing beside him and talking to him. 'But he didn't look like Rob as a man,' said Jon, 'he was just a boy. And I held his hand.'

Jon was on the verge of tears and apologised for this stream of consciousness that he'd just shared with the group, but he didn't need to say sorry.

We all knew what he was trying to say. That Rob had so much bravado, he was so cocky and fun. But, when you took away the jokes and the swagger and looked at him, I mean *really* looked at him, you finally saw how fragile he was. He may have looked like a man and talked like a man. But he never learned how to move past the fears and vulnerabilities he had as a boy.

After Rob died, lots of people said, like Jon, that they dreamed about him. I was so jealous. I didn't dream about Rob, except rarely, and, when I did, it always revolved around him being an addict and I *always* knew he was dead in the dream. Even now.

I found out about these dreams because people posted them on Facebook. They wrote about their feelings, letters to Rob, recalled stories that were wonderful – things we, family and friends, didn't know about and brought our man back to life briefly. Some of it was great, some of it wasn't. Some of it was way too personal and inappropriate.

Never in my wildest imaginings did I think I'd have to

factor in social media while grieving. When the great author Joan Didion penned a book about losing her husband, she didn't write: 'And then I wondered whether or not to cancel John's Facebook account.'

But a lot of grief is not pragmatic. It's emotional, and Facebook is one of those tools people use to communicate that emotion, which often feels out of control, messy and dramatic.

Perhaps I was tetchy about Facebook for other reasons. Shortly before Rob died, he deleted his account, or so we thought. After a suicide, you search for any level of detail that might indicate how serious the person was about taking their own life. Rob left no will, never spoke to me about the type of funeral he would want, and didn't leave any of his affairs in order.

But he deleted his Facebook account before he died. And he killed himself by hanging, which is a method people choose if they really mean to go through with it. So that must have meant some element of planning went into his death, right?

Imagine our shock, our fright, when for some unknown reason the Facebook account resurrected itself four months after his death like a digital Jesus.

I looked on his account and saw that two weeks before his death, he had chosen a photo of us as his profile picture. In the last two months before his death he posted selfies in which he looked very, very ill. There is one photo that is extremely hard to look at – he's facing the camera but looking down with his head in his hands, tired, fed up. Everything about it says, *I want peace.*

When the account came back up, people immediately started posting messages to him, which I found ridiculous. I was tempted to take down the account. Wherever Rob was, he wasn't on Facebook.

But then I realised that many of these people had not been able to visit his grave because it was in Auckland. So, as far-fetched as it sounds, and perhaps I am giving Mark Zuckerberg's creation far too much importance, for some people this was the grave. This was the altar at which they could lay their thoughts and pictures and feel that, somehow, they were touching a part of Rob through one of the last remnants of himself he had left behind.

So much of what makes a person who they were is intangible, but this was the wisp of smoke frozen in a moment. Now, when someone posts something I don't like, I just view it as them bringing flowers I don't like to his grave. (Calla lilies, FYI.)

A rare dream about Rob, a year after his death. We're in bed and he's so sleepy.

He's at the stage where his body is physically withdrawing from drug use; there are lines around his eyes, which hang heavy in his head, as if he's been through a long journey across a desert.

But although he's lying prone and half-awake, I throw my arms over him and hold him tight. I know what is going to happen. Someone has already told me the end of this story.

'Please don't go,' I say. 'Please don't go. Please don't go.'

'Hmm?' Rob replies, sleepily. 'I'm not going anywhere, honey.'

But I know that he is. I know that, soon, he will fall into an inky blackness so deep he will not be able to find his way back. Soon, he will reach the point where he won't have the choice of turning back, and slowly he will move to a place where we can't reach him, where he is lost to us forever.

'Please, Rob. Please don't go.' The sharpness of the wish, the desperation streaming from my eyes, is like a knife sliding from my throat to my stomach.

It lays everything bare, and there is never a moment when I feel as powerless as when I am trying to call my husband back from the land of the dead. I have to find peace in all of this; I must, or I am afraid I will join him.

At night, when I look at the sky, I wonder what frequency our grief resonates at.

All those people, around the world, who spend those quiet moments silently calling the dead back to them.

There comes a point when I realise the dead cannot come back, ever.

It doesn't matter that I sleep in our old bed. Or that I refuse to move any of the paintings he hung up. Or that I can't move out of the flat we lived in together.

What am I holding on to? None of that is going to bring him back.

I close my eyes and I think of the twelve men who will die that day by their own hand. And the next day. I know this number will tick on and on, unless we stop calling to the dead and instead decide to turn our gaze towards the living.

# Chapter Fourteen

I watch a programme called *Suicide and Me*, by the musician Professor Green, aka Stephen Manderson, who lost his father to suicide at a young age.

It features a tiny place in north London, a sanctuary that has an exceptionally high success rate at helping people who are on the verge of suicide. A person can stay there for five days, and once they leave, they can't return. But for many people, once is enough. It has saved over a thousand lives, and it currently is the only one of its kind in Britain.

I found Maytree. Its director, Natalie, and I are sitting in a restaurant near my office. I stir my coffee, and I ask her about prevention.

Like Mr B, she's of the firm belief that unless we start teaching children about emotional intelligence, we are simply firefighting.

Maytree have done something very clever: they have put

content on their website that means when someone Googles 'want to kill myself', their site comes up at the top of the search, which is literally a lifeline to someone at the end of their road.

Although there are people who have come to Natalie's door because they've suffered horrific childhood abuse or have severe mental illness, there are also those with 'perfectly normal upbringings' who have found themselves in a perfect storm. One such person, who came to them after searching for ways to kill himself, was an ex-serviceman who'd been in Afghanistan.

'He had seen things that you shouldn't see,' Natalie said. 'He came back and was discharged, so he'd lost his sense of purpose, but also structure. And that obviously impacted on his mental wellbeing and relationship with his wife. His wife went and had an affair, they got divorced, that was ugly and there were children involved.

'So there was this knock-on effect and he just couldn't cope any more. He didn't want to die; he just couldn't see how he could continue with his life.'

The structure of Maytree is remarkably simple. Its job is to provide a safe, calm space where people won't be judged. It is built utterly on trust, from the moment they call to the moment they leave.

'It's also a model delivered by volunteers,' said Natalie. 'So let's say within the NHS you are depressed and you get assigned a psychiatrist. What if you don't connect with that psychiatrist, what if there is no trust? How do you expect that relationship to evolve into something supportive and fruitful?

'So in Maytree, a guest will see, in one day, about twelve different volunteers. Out of those, that individual will connect with at least one or two of them. And the feedback we get from guests is that the fact that someone they've never met before is willing to give up their time for nothing and spend it with [them] reinstates that they are worth it. Because a lot of the time, that individual's self-esteem, by the time they come to us, is flat on the floor.

'That a complete stranger is willing to sit with them, and not judge or try to change or fix their darkest thoughts and feelings – it plants the seeds of what was maybe there before. Which is: I am worth the time, I am worth fighting for. I am worth spending time with. And that is the seed of hope.'

Natalie can't read my mind. But I am overcome at the work she does, and I think of all of those families who still have their loved ones because of her and Maytree.

Here is a model that works. And so I pledge that I will do whatever I can to help her.

I finally feel like Rob's legacy is taking shape.

# Afterword

Life is moving forward.

I have been speaking publically about mental health and suicide and writing regularly about suicide prevention, and a doctor friend of mine told me that, after reading my blog about Rob, she spearheaded a major mental health pilot scheme to create better understanding between patients and professionals.

I've decided other parts of my life have to change.

Although it took a long time to get to the point where I didn't want to throw up at the idea, I've tentatively started dating again after I realised voluntary celibacy probably wasn't my thing.

I realise that I must be a difficult person to love right now, or for someone to want to be with, connect with. Deep down, there is a vast room and in it are all the memories I have with Rob. In this room, he is alive and I am in love.

And the man it would take to hold my hand and say *I*

*love you, and I know you have that room and I love that room*
*because it makes you* you, *and I can hold both you and Rob in*
*my heart* . . . that man – does he even exist? That man would
have to be a greater person than me. I don't know if he will
ever make his way to me. But I've been through enough to
know I'll be okay if he doesn't.

I have bought my first ever apartment, and I've finally gone
through the boxes of Rob's possessions – though it took a lot
of red wine, tissues and James Taylor.

To mark the end of summer, Martin invites me to come to
France, exactly a year after my last trip. It's a welcome respite
from packing up my house.

The last time I was here, it was two months after Rob died
and Martin wanted to give me somewhere restful to stay. He
cooked, we went for long walks and it was what I needed.

At the time I felt very fragile, so one morning, instead of a
walk, I went for a run to clear my head. I passed dark green
hedges, open fields filled with white flowers dotted across like
a meadow of falling stars.

Then I came across a woodland, tall conifers radiating
from the dark heart of the forest. I thought of Rob, I felt his
death pass through me, and I couldn't run any more because
I was crying so hard.

This time round, I decide again to go for a run in the cool
morning before it gets too hot.

I pass the same forest, but it is breathtaking how different
I feel. How much stronger I am. How I am able to hold Rob

close, but not feel like the memory of him will drown me. I never believed a day would come when I could feel like this, but it has happened and, finally, I am turning with the world.

In the distance, I see a field of sweetcorn, green, unripe ears pointing upwards. They bend and sway in the breeze. I don't know why I do this, but I leave the roadside and push my way through the field so that, soon, I am lost in corn.

It whispers and rustles around me with the bluest sky overhead and, after a time, my breathing slows, and I feel like I am watching the earth grow.

Although there are barely any clouds visible, from nowhere a brief shower of rain passes overhead. And when it stops, in the bright glow of the summer sun, a mighty rainbow arches across the sky, a fiery arrow shot from another world to mine.

*Rob.*

I'm crying, but I'm laughing, and I sincerely hope that no one can see this small, crazy Indian girl crying and laughing in the middle of a field of sweetcorn.

*I love you, I love you,* I say to the sky and to the earth. *A thousand times, I love you.*

# *Endnotes*

1. http://www.vice.com/read/why-are-your-dreams-suddenly-so-intense-when-you-stop-smoking-weed-876
2. http://www.huffingtonpost.co.uk/jamie-flexman/depression-mental-illness_b_3931629.html
3. https://www.gov.uk/government/uploads/system/uploads/attachment_data/file/462885/drug-misuse-1415.pdf
4. http://www.independent.co.uk/news/uk/crime/uk-is-the-addiction-capital-of-europe-report-claims-8793170.html
5. http://time.com/3946904/heroin-epidemic/
6. https://www.ted.com/talks/johann_hari_everything_you_think_you_know_about_addiction_is_wrong/transcript?language=en
7. https://www.rsph.org.uk/our-work/policy/protecting-the-public-s-health/taking-a-new-line-on-drugs.html
8. http://www.huffingtonpost.com/johann-hari/7-facts-about-drugs-that-will-make-you-question-everything_b_9484744.html

# Useful Books and Organisations

*Cry of Pain: Understanding Suicide and the Suicidal Mind*,
  Professor Mark Williams (Piatkus, 2014)
*Notes on Suicide*, Simon Critchley (Fitzcarraldo Editions, 2015)

CALM (Campaign Against Living Miserably) helps
prevention of suicide among men
0800 58 58 58
https://www.thecalmzone.net/

MIND is the leading UK mental health charity
0300 123 3393
http://www.mind.org.uk/

The Samaritans provide a listening service
116 123
http://www.samaritans.org/

The Listening Place offers a safe environment in London where people who are feeling suicidal can make an appointment to come and talk to someone
http://listeningplace.org.uk/

Maytree is a sanctuary for the suicidal in London with a high success rate
0207 263 7070
http://www.maytree.org.uk/

Lifeline is a UK-wide charity that helps people and families affected by drug and alcohol addiction
0161 200 5486
http://www.lifeline.org.uk/

# Acknowledgements

Mum and Dad, everything I have learned about compassion, kindness and helping other people has come from you. This book would not have been possible without you, and there are no words sufficient to express how proud I am to be yours, and how much dignity your unfailing love has given me.

Prue and David – I was lucky enough to have one set of phenomenal parents, but through Rob, I gained another. The word *aroha* may have started with him, but it continues with you. I cannot thank you enough for the love you have shown me, and for giving me your blessing to write about our beloved boy.

Priya, we have always had a language beyond words because we are sisters – thank you for the hugs when I wasn't able to speak and endless cups of tea. John and Alan, you are my brothers for life and thank you for calling me your sister.

To the fabulous duo who Rob described as 'The

Aunties' – Gabrielle and Felicity – who gave me strength and confidence to write this book.

To Mal – who has always had faith in me, and who undertook the hardest of journeys with me. I can never repay you for holding my hand in the darkest of moments. You are more than my friend, you are family. Jesse, brother: you were there for him in life, you were there for him in death, and it means so much that you brought him alive for this book.

For Hasiba, whose love and companionship stopped me from drowning in the first year. For Martin, who opened his heart and home to me when I needed time and space to write. For my boys Niaz, Kumaran and Ahmed, who have always been able to make me laugh when I needed it most. For all of my friends and family who kept me afloat with their love – Karen, Tania, Shabby, Prarthana, James, George, Rashme, Poonam, Sonia, Alice, Gun, Shwetha, Aarti, Jools, Anoushka, Monique.

To Rob's New Zealand crew, whose messages kept me going in moments of despair – David M, Wesley, Malcolm, Amanda, the Arnolds and the wonderful Louise.

I wouldn't have been able to write this book if I hadn't been so well supported at work, and so a huge thank you goes to Brogan, Stephen and Ellen, who saved me in so many ways they probably don't know about.

To my agent Rowan at Furniss Lawton, who I knew was The One when I met her, who just 'got it' and treated this book with utmost respect. To my editor Nicki at Simon &

Schuster, for her sensitivity, her faith and words of support. To Nikki and Izzy, for their invaluable advice and affection. Isobel H, for keeping me sane.

And just a huge thank you to everyone who ever wrote a kind comment under one of my pieces about Rob, who reached out and emailed me after I wrote my blog at a time when I felt barely tethered to this world. You helped keep me here, and inspired this book.